LIVING BEYOND THE LIMITS

LIVING BEYOND THE LIMITS

A Life in Sync with God

Franklin Graham

THOMAS NELSON PUBLISHERS
Nashville

Published in Nashville, Tennessee,
by Thomas Nelson, Inc., Publishers.

Library of Congress Cataloging-in-Publication Data
Graham, Franklin, 1952–
Living beyond the limits / Franklin Graham.
p.   cm.
ISBN 0-7852-7184-8 (hardcover)
1. Christian life. 2. Graham, Franklin, 1952–
3. Christian biography. I. Title
BV4501.2.G72455   1998
248.4—dc21
98-11788
CIP

Printed in the United States of America.
1 2 3 4 5 6 BVG 03 02 01 00 99 98

*This book is dedicated to my mother and father
who have been an example and inspiration to me.*

TABLE OF CONTENTS

ACKNOWLEDGMENTS

GOD SENDS MANY PEOPLE along life's pathway to help and encourage us. Gary Thomas is one of those professionals who came across my path when I began this book. He is one of those talented writers who spent hours working with me, taping these chapters and putting them in a format that made sense. Thank you, Gary. I'd work with you anytime.

To my friend Preston Parrish who reviewed each chapter and gave insightful suggestions—thanks, buddy.

To Russ Busby who read the manuscript early on and gave me his honest opinions—thanks.

To my mother who read these pages and edited out what she didn't like—I love you.

To Elizabeth Kaye who read the manuscript carefully and made invaluable comments from start to finish—I'm grateful for the time you freely offered.

To my secretary, Donna Lee Toney, who spent hours incorporating everyone's changes and suggestions, and at times gave her own valuable insights that have strengthened many pages of this book.

To Bruce Nygren who didn't help one bit on this project. However, I hope you can help me on the next one—I missed you.

To Rolf Zettersten, Janet Thoma, and the entire Thomas Nelson team, thank you. You are a delight to work with. This project could not have been done without your help and support.

ALL MY LIFE, I've loved machines that are fast, loud, even dangerous. That's just the way I am. Whether it's flying an airplane, riding the wind on a dirt bike, four-wheeling through the Colorado mountains, or cruising in my old pickup through the North Carolina countryside, I love it! What I don't love are roller coasters or carnival Ferris wheels, especially when they start down. I'd much rather be in the cockpit twenty thousand feet up in the clouds than sitting in a chair forty feet above the ground with someone else at the controls.

Maybe that is why, as a young man, I was so reluctant to surrender my life to God. I thought Christianity would be boring, that it would mean living by other people's dull rules, that it would be, in a sense, a living death. I wanted to be in complete control. I wanted to live hard, fast, and free, to experience life on the edge.

And for a while, I did. I witnessed firsthand what it was like to hear bullets whizzing past my head and artillery exploding in the distance. I crossed closely guarded borders and traveled over perilous and exotic terrain.

But eventually the excitement proved to be nothing more than a temporary high. I soon realized that there wasn't enough adventure in the entire world to satisfy my thirsty spirit. No matter how thrilling the day, when my head hit the pillow at night I was overcome by a nagging emptiness—a dark void.

I began to discover what King Solomon lamented in the book of Ecclesiastes: *"I denied myself nothing my eyes desired; I refused my heart no pleasure. . . . Yet when I surveyed all that my hands had done and what I had toiled to achieve, everything was meaningless, a chasing after the wind; . . . So I hated life. . . . All of it is meaningless"* (2:10–11,17 NIV).

As my teen years dissolved into my early twenties, I began meeting people who lived exhilarating lives—but curiously, without the shallowness that plagued my own. These people were full of life. Their eyes sparkled with the energy that flowed through them. As I probed the reason for their peace and zest for life, I discovered that they all had a common thread woven integrally through their lives. They had made decisions to bring an unusual Person into their lives, a Man whom so much of history has been centered around. That Man is Jesus Christ, God's Son.

They were not the type of Christians who fell asleep in the back pews, mind you. They were Christians who lived on the cutting edge, where their faith looked boldly into the face of a sin-sick world. They had found the master key to synchronizing their lives with God's will. By doing so, they had been set on an adventuresome pathway. These men and women had daring courage, deep conviction, and devoted commitment. The result: They were living life to its fullest; they embodied hope, promise, and an eagerness to serve God.

As soul-seekers on life's fast-paced highways, they looked for those who were lost along the way.

The time I spent with these folks made me want what they had. Still, the thought of giving up control of my life went against my grain—like a teenager having to turn his car keys over to his dad!

But one night, after years of searching, I came to the same conclusion as King Solomon—everything was meaningless. I was on a road whose end was destruction. I finally asked God to forgive me for my sins and rebellion. I asked Jesus Christ to come into my heart and be the Lord of my life. That very night He gave me total peace. The black, empty hole that engulfed my life was filled with a powerful sense of direction. I found the will to pick up the pieces and move on, but now in sync with Him. Immediately, my life began to change.

You talk about a high! Oh sure, there were some struggles. But now I knew where my source of strength was—and I tapped into it. It didn't take me long to learn that I had embarked on the ultimate trip—to pursue the path set in place for me by the Creator of all life, and to serve the King of all kings. Not only could I throw myself into an adventurous life in confidence, despite its unknown challenges, but I could do so for a cause bigger than myself, to help others step out of the shameful and dark side of life and exchange it for the lasting peace of walking with the Savior.

It's been over two decades since I've given my heart to Jesus Christ, over two decades of following in Christ's footsteps, over two decades of watching the hand of the Almighty move in my life and around the world. Along the journey I have met people who, with grit and sheer gutsiness for God, have found lasting satisfaction and made a difference.

I have also learned something else. While all of us need a good start in life, it also matters how we make the journey and how we finish.

I love to fly airplanes, especially the Mitsubishi MU2. The MU2 is fast—known in the aviation industry as "the rice rocket." It will get me where I need to go really quick. The MU2 is one of the best turboprops ever built but, strangely enough, it was never a favorite among pilots. One of the reasons, I guess, is that it's a difficult plane to fly.

In the Christian life, just like in a plane, you need a good take-off—salvation in Jesus Christ. But just as important, you want to be able to fly safely, navigate around the storms, and eventually land at the ultimate destination without crashing. Ideally, you want to make those wheels touch down on the runway without one single bump.

The Christian life is a long-term, lifelong trip, and the Bible warns us of those who seem to get a good start but then stray or falter.

A lot of people could get an MU2 up in the air, but flying it on course and getting it down safely is a bit tougher. Once we come to God His way, we need the proper knowledge and training along with additional instruction and experience in order to keep flying. Regardless of life's storms, temptations, and challenges, we all want to finish well.

During flight training for the MU2, my instructor, Reece Howell of Howell Enterprises, will do his best to test my skills to the limit. He straps me into the cockpit, gets me thousands of feet up in the air, and then throws at me every emergency imaginable, one after another, and sometimes all at once. Whether an electrical problem or a simulated power failure, there is a detailed procedure on the emergency checklist that explains how to handle each and every situation, and the instructor expects me to figure out the right steps to take to correct the problem.

Whether you are a coal miner from the hollers of West Virginia, or a neurosurgeon practicing at the University of California, you might want to consider this book "flight training" for your journey. It's a refresher course for how we can keep in step with God, surviving even under the most adverse conditions. Instead of an electrical failure, we'll simulate what it's like to face our biggest fears as we walk with God through the uncertainties of life. Instead of studying the ins and outs of cockpit instruments and landing gears, we'll explore what it's like to stay in sync with God.

An essential part of flying any multiengine airplane well is making sure the engines are finely tuned and that the propellers are passing the fuselage in sync. You won't crash if the propellers aren't just right; you can still fly the plane, but there will be that little bit of irritation, that slight noise, that uncomfortable and fatiguing vibration—and by the time you reach your destination, you'll be exhausted from the constant tremor.

I am sure that all of us have encountered times in our lives when we felt out of sync with God, not crashing, just simply in a spiritual holding pattern—faithful in tithing to the church and faithful in providing for our families. In other words, doing all the right things yet still feeling that slight pulsation quivering right under the surface of our conscience.

Instead of joy and fulfillment, many people feel exhausted and depressed. They have lost hope and settled in for a tiresome and mundane life. Something is missing. Their compass is out of calibration and is beyond its boundaries. Their lives are not in sync with God.

Do you feel out of sync? Feeling that constant subtle vibration? About to go crazy at times? Do you wish you could find the instruction and insight necessary to live life to its fullest, so your heart can beat with God's?

Life is a journey as we travel through this world, and we need all the help we can get. In the following pages, I would like to introduce you to some people whom God has used in my life. I trust that you will experience a refreshing reminder of the exciting and adventurous life of faith in Jesus Christ.

FACING YOUR FEARS

I WAS SHAKEN FROM MY SLEEP by the rapid sound of machine-gun fire. *What in the world am I doing here?"* I asked my first night in the heart of Africa's Angola. From the beginning of this trip, I had struggled with a strong sense of foreboding, and now I couldn't shake a sinking feeling in my stomach. The incessant clatter of machine guns and the accompanying sounds of breaking glass, shouting men, and another ripping blast from the muzzle of a Russian AK-47 once again shattered the momentary silence and made it impossible to go back to sleep.

I knew it, I thought. *I knew I'd end up dying in this place.*

I was drawn to war-torn Angola in the early eighties through the invitation of Dr. Steve Duncan. I met him while speaking at a missions conference in Florida. Steve was a well-educated Boston man and a skilled surgeon. He was preparing to leave for Angola as soon as he could raise support and make the logistical arrangements.

Steve made quite an impression on me as he told of his desire to serve the Lord in a foreign country. I knew he could be earning enough money to buy anybody's version of the great American Dream. Instead, all he talked about was taking God's gospel to Angola—a country that at the time was in the throes of a particularly vicious and ugly civil war.

In fact, it was more than just a civil war; Angola was the African focal point of the Cold War. Angola was Marxist, supported by the Soviet Union with thousands of Russian advisers and their Cuban proxies. The rebels, known as UNITA (Union for Total Independence of Angola), were led by a freedom fighter known as Jonas Savimbi and supported by South Africa, the United States, and others.

"Franklin," Steve challenged me, "when I get to Angola, why don't you come visit me?"

"Sure," I answered, much too quickly.

Have you ever said something for the sake of being polite? As I walked away, the delighted look on his face as he heard my answer tugged at my conscience. I thought, *Surely he wouldn't really expect me to go to Angola, of all places!*

When Can You Make It?

Not only is Steve Duncan a committed doctor, he has a remarkable memory, as I discovered a year later.

In the early years of my ministry at Samaritan's Purse, I always liked to shuffle through the morning mail—still do when I'm in the office. I found the variety of envelopes intriguing—the foreign postage stamps, the onion-thin paper with postmarks from exotic corners of the earth. I was amazed that they could make it that far. Many times over the years, a letter or phone call has determined what path my day will take. So it was quite natural, one morning, for me to slice open an envelope stamped LUANDA, ANGOLA. I unfolded the letter and with astonishment read:

> "Hi, Franklin. I'm here. When are you coming to Angola? Do you remember your promise to come? When can you make it?"

Do I remember?

The letter became heavy as my hand hit the desk, and the grin dropped from my face. *He remembered,* I thought. *No way on God's green earth do I want to go. Angola is in the midst of civil war. I don't want to get mixed up in that mess.*

CNN wasn't covering the war up close, but reports of Cuban pilots flying Russian planes bombing cities and villages still managed to leak out of the country. Indescribable destruction littered the countryside. Warring factions had chased every reliable airline out of the country, mined the roads, and demolished many bridges. There were even some reports of biological weapons and chemical gases.

I threw the letter into a heap on my secretary's desk and fumbled for something that would better fit into my plan. But I really couldn't concentrate on anything. Throughout the day I found myself reaching for Steve's letter—like a magnet I couldn't get away from. As I juggled phone calls and various business matters, Steve Duncan's face kept coming to mind. I caught myself studying the wall map in my office. I thought about his determination and dedication to proclaim the gospel of Jesus Christ through missionary medicine in an extremely volatile part of the world. No matter how hard I tried to deny it, I knew I had to live up to the promise I had made.

As the day raced down an uncertain path, I found myself formulating a possible plan to go to Africa. From a practical perspective, it could take me a week or more to get into Angola. After all, the only transportation within the country was handled by TAG Airlines. I wondered if it stood for "Tag, you're it—you'll be blown up next!" Hostages were being snatched around the world with a frightening regularity, and I had no desire to become tomorrow's headline. If I traveled to Angola, I would be on my own, with no assurance of ever getting out alive. I sure couldn't count on the U.S. State Department to come to my rescue if I got trapped. They were emphatically warning Americans to stay out.

Steve's example of determination and commitment convicted me. Jesus told His disciples to go into all the world—not just the pleasant places. After careful thought and prayer, it seemed that all of my excuses not to go were as thin as the paper Steve had written on. I couldn't rid the discontent until I wired Steve and told him that I believed God was leading me to go. I hadn't been beaten over the head. It was simply that "still, small voice" that made it clear to me that God was calling me to go to Angola, and that He used Steve's letter to get that message through.

I called a pastor friend of mine from Arizona. "Guy, how about going with me to Angola?" He laughed, figuring I must be joking. I told him about my letter from Steve Duncan. To my surprise he said, "Sure, I'll go, when do we leave?"

As I began making final preparations, I couldn't shake the ominous sense that once I left I might never plant my feet on American soil again. The battle within convinced me to hold out a fleece.

For those of you who are not familiar with the biblical story of fleeces, Gideon, an Old Testament hero, used two fleeces to double check the will of God concerning His command to lead an army to battle. The first time, Gideon placed a wool fleece on a threshing floor and prayed to God: *"Look, I shall put a fleece of wool on the threshing floor; if there is dew on the fleece only, and it is dry on all the ground, then I shall know that You will save Israel by my hand, as You have said"* (Judg. 6:37).

The next morning, Gideon got up and squeezed enough water out of the fleece to fill a bowl. But that wasn't enough for Gideon. He laid out another fleece and prayed: *"Do not be angry with me, but let me speak just once more: Let me test, I pray, just once more with the fleece; let it now be dry only on the fleece, but on all the ground let there be dew"* (Judg. 6:39).

When morning came, it was just as Gideon had asked. He could no longer pretend that God wasn't leading him into battle.

I felt like Gideon—fairly certain that I should go, but not at all pleased with the direction I was headed. *Just in case,* I said to myself, *I'm gonna give God a chance to close the door and keep me at home.*

"Lord," I prayed, "if You don't want me to go, then when I get down to Charlotte, cause Piedmont Airlines to be late so that I'll miss my plane in New York." I had a very tight connection in New York. If the airline was more than a few minutes late, it wouldn't be possible for me to catch my next flight. Preston Parrish, a friend who was working with me at the time, met me at the airport and we boarded the plane—right on time.

When Piedmont Airlines pushed back a few minutes ahead of schedule, I was sure it was the first early departure in their history, and I thought of Gideon's bowl of water. As soon as the plane was airborne, I prayed, "God, if it's really not Your will for us to go to Angola right now, let there be bad weather, maybe even a thunderstorm, forcing the plane to circle New York. That way, we'll miss our plane to Paris."

We got into New York *before* our scheduled arrival time. Preston and I found Guy waiting for us. It was one of the most stress-less connections I had ever made.

By now, I was really concerned.

I figured a third fleece might make a difference. "Okay, Lord," I prayed as our plane crossed the Atlantic, "This is the last chance." At that time of year Paris could get fogged in. "If You don't want us to go to Angola, send a thick fog so the plane can't land. We'll miss our connection in Paris and take it as Your will that we're not supposed to go on to Angola."

After hours of restless sleep on the plane, a voice came over the speaker saying that we would be landing in Paris soon. I raised the window shade and looked out into the most beautiful, cloudless sky I had ever seen. The city—and the airport's runways—were in clear view.

It finally sunk in. I was really on my way to Angola.

A LONG NIGHT

The passengers who boarded the plane in Paris intrigued me. As I looked around the cabin I wondered who these people were. Many looked as though they might be mercenaries or adventurers from Eastern Europe, Romania, or Bulgaria. Some looked like they could have been spies out of a James Bond movie—it was an eerie feeling.

We arrived at Luanda, Angola's international airport, late in the evening. As we got off the plane, the military advisers from the Soviet bloc who had been on board were warmly greeted with hugs and kisses from their Angolan hosts. Their presence only heightened our sense of being on the edge of an abyss. This huge airport terminal was lit by just a few lightbulbs that hung from the ceiling on bare wires. The lack of adequate lighting contributed to the fear that was welling up inside. We had descended into a world of shadows. It was a weird feeling for this country boy accustomed to wide-open spaces lit by the sun's brilliance.

We did our best to make our way toward the cubicle that served as the immigration office. One tiny lightbulb threw its faint glow onto the counter of the officer, who, to my dismay, was solely responsible for admitting a planeload of passengers.

I took one look at the long line and thought, *It's going to take all night to be processed.* The only consolation was that morning would bring some natural light—maybe then we could see our way around.

The airport was full of Africans whose native tongue was Portuguese, a language neither my friends nor I spoke. My eyes strained through the dim light hoping to catch a glimpse of Steve Duncan, but he was nowhere in sight. *Maybe the war has prevented him from being able to meet us.*

Because the thought of tourists flying into the midst of civil war was ludicrous, the police and soldiers were suspicious of our presence—why would Americans come to Luanda? The language gap made it almost impossible to explain our intentions. To make matters worse, the United States was supporting the guerrilla army in the civil war, but the Soviet-backed government operated the international airport. I couldn't help but wonder if one more fleece would have changed my course.

Standing behind the desk, in the shadows, were the Cuban secret police, who monitored all arrivals into the country. *This could get ugly, real quick,* I thought as I sensed them staring at us. I had imagined an accident, a shelling, an ambush, a land mine, or some other horrible tragedy here in Angola, but the Cuban secret police—that hadn't occurred to me. I began to ponder what death by torture would be like.

As I stood waiting to be called, I rehearsed what I would say to the officer. When I finally approached the immigration desk, I reluctantly handed over my American passport. With a few steps forward, the Cuban official emerged from the shadows, curious about why I was there. When the immigration officer spoke to me in Portuguese, I shrugged my shoulders and made a feeble attempt to answer in English. I think my Southern accent confused him.

Out of the darkness came a welcome sound, "Glad you made it, Franklin." I looked toward the voice, and there stood Dr. Steve Duncan like an angel at the midnight hour. He was grinnin' from ear to ear. "I've got your visas." He waved them in the air.

Suddenly a sense of peace came over me—and I even thought for a few minutes that everything was going to be all right. Steve handed the authorized documents to the officer and rattled off an explanation in Portuguese, like it was his mother tongue. The Cuban policeman quickly faded into the shadows, and with no further suspense, the officer plastered the entry visas into our passports and cleared us through the system.

Steve slapped me on the back and said, "Franklin, I knew you'd come. Let's get goin'."

As long as that meant "let's get out of here," I was all for it. When I saw Steve's face, the doubts I had about the trip disappeared, and I was assured that the right decision had been made.

When we left the airport we headed straight for a high-rise apartment complex that had been caught in its share of combat. The elevator didn't work, there was no electricity, and sewage ran down the stairs. We had to carry our bags up seven flights of steps in the dark. When we got to the sixth floor, Steve shouted, "Be careful!" pointing to a huge hole directly in front of us. A good portion of the landing was gone, leaving a dangerous hole that would have swallowed us up if we had been misguided. I couldn't believe it! There were no flags or signs warning of the hazard; Steve had just learned to count the number of floors in the darkness.

The small apartment we were to stay in belonged to an older missionary couple who frequently opened up their home to others coming through. They gave Steve and Preston the corner of the living room and then ushered Guy and me to the master suite. *Boy, have we lucked out*, I thought. They opened the door, and the sight took my breath away. There was one single cot pushed up against the wall of a tiny storage closet. The smell of gasoline was intense. It was no wonder, when I finally spotted the fifty-five-gallon drums over in the corner. Gasoline is at a premium during a war, so these missionaries had no choice but to maintain a stock of precious fuel.

The man and his wife apologized for not having more than one cot, and then said good night. I cracked the door open and glanced into the other room, wondering if I could talk Preston into trading places. Maybe I could persuade him that he would have more privacy in my room. But then again, maybe not. I closed the door and looked at Guy staring at that flimsy single cot that two grown men were supposed to share. I broke the somber moment and laughingly said, "So, where are you going to sleep?" Guy fumbled frantically for his airline guide, looking for the next flight out. I tried to encourage him that we could make the best of a bad situation. Besides, we were bone tired.

We climbed into the squeaky cot and tucked in the mosquito net. Then I laid down the ground rules. "Here's the middle of the bed," I told him. "You take your half, and I'll take my mine. Don't you dare let a toenail cross this line."

We tried desperately to go to sleep but were so self-conscious about moving one way or the other that not a muscle relaxed. I thought, *This is crazy. We're in a city ravaged by civil war and random gunshots, on a cot surrounded by gallons of gasoline!*

Suddenly, machine-gun fire ripped the veil of silence. Immediately, I thought of the gasoline.

Guy broke the lull between us.

"I'm catching the next plane out," he said in a dead whisper.

"We are already scheduled on the next plane out," I snapped. "And that flight leaves a week from now."

Dejected, he carefully rolled over and mumbled.

The long night eased into a welcome sunrise, even though we were still in the dark as to how we were going to get to our destination—Lubango—800 miles to the south. We sure couldn't go by car. It was far too risky, as there were ambushes nearly every day. Our hosts greeted us with a quick breakfast, hot coffee, and some very good news. "You'll be able to catch a flight to the little town of Moçâmedes," they told us, "then you'll have only a four-hour drive to Lubango."

We packed our gear, thanked this sweet couple, and headed back to the airport. There was plenty of light now, and the sun was beating down with a blistering heat. We walked into a grimy, sweaty, hot free-for-all. It seemed everyone was fearful of the mined roads, so the airport was jammed with wanna-be passengers, hoping like us to fly out of this mess. I was willing to risk getting shot out of the air rather than chancing an ambush. That is, until I looked out on the tarmac and gazed upon a sorry excuse for a jet.

One look at the dilapidated plane and I thought, *What kind of maintenance, if any, has this pitiful engine gone through?*

Steve was right with us, encouraging us. "Oh, it will be okay," he said, leaving us momentarily to see if he could get tickets. As if not skeptical enough, I overheard someone say in English, "There used to be five planes, but this is the only one left; the others got shot down." We stood looking in disbelief as Steve walked up and pulled out four airline tickets and smiled. "Good news! We got on." And minutes later we boarded the flight.

I listened as the crew fired up the engines, wondering if we would ever make it back home. I looked around at the sweaty passengers carrying their produce and live chickens. Other than the horrendous smell, the flight was uneventful and rather smooth. As we began to descend, I spotted the little landing strip out in the middle of a forsaken and scorched expanse.

We deplaned right where we landed. There was no terminal for shelter—just a hut—and worse, there was no one to meet us. I looked at Steve but didn't say a word. Here we stood in the middle of nowhere, with no food or water, no taxi service, and no clue how to get to our destination. The other passengers quickly grabbed their baggage, which had been dumped in the middle of the tarmac, and jumped into old buses and the backs of pickup trucks. No one hung around—not even the guards. By the time the plane roared off into the distance, the airport was deserted.

With hands in our pockets, we stood at the empty airport, looking down the road to the right, then to the left. Somehow from out of nowhere two African men appeared, saw our despondent faces, and asked, "Can we help you?"

"A friend was supposed to meet us here," Steve explained. "He should have been here by now."

"We'll take you to town when our ride comes. It'll be here soon," one said.

We felt the rays of the late afternoon sun burning our skin and quickly took them up on their offer.

Saved by a Dump Truck

The air was so still and quiet. There wasn't much else to do other than watch the lonely road. Before long we noticed a huge cloud of dust rising up to cloak what looked like a big, white dump truck.

"Here comes our ride!" one of the strangers shouted as we heard the thud of the wheels hitting the potholes. We threw our bags and fatigued bodies into the dirty bed of the truck as it slowly rolled to a stop. Then we grabbed the side of the rusty vehicle, hanging on for dear life as the driver hit the accelerator full force. Our body weight and luggage couldn't quite compare to the twenty or thirty tons the truck was designed to carry. It bounced and clattered as the steel bed slapped against the frame. The noise alone was deafening, but that wasn't as bad as the cloud of dust that engulfed us. With every breath, we choked on the gritty air that filled our lungs.

Even so, we didn't complain. We were thankful to have only five miles to travel to reach some measure of civilization.

As we approached the outskirts of town we glared through the dusty glass of every vehicle that passed us, hoping to connect with Steve's friend. Off in the distance, he noticed a white Chevrolet Suburban barreling toward us. Steve banged on the cab of the truck. "Stop!" The driver locked the brakes, and we skidded to a standstill just about the time Steve's friend screeched to a halt.

When we looked across the road, the driver was none other than Steve Duncan's friend from Lubango, Dr. Steve Foster, who was a missionary doctor as well. He rolled the window down and greeted us. His thick, lamb-chop sideburns bristled up when he flashed his trademark grin the size of Africa.

We jumped over the side of the truck, thanked our African friends for their help, and piled into Dr. Foster's Suburban.

We learned that Dr. Foster not only operated on his patients using exceptional techniques, he had done a nice piece of work on this fine set of wheels.

His vehicle was a bit out of the ordinary. He had modified it for protection from the land mines buried dangerously underground. First, he jacked it up by six extra inches. Underneath the body, he had fabricated a two-inch thick aluminum ballistics-grade plate. His theory was, if he ran over a land mine, the plate would absorb the blast. The car might be blown off the road, but he'd probably survive.

That was his theory, at least.

As we drove farther on, Dr. Foster pointed out the guerrilla soldiers' encampments alongside the road. "That's the ANC (African National Congress)", he said, "suspiciously guarded by Cubans and East Germans." Dr. Foster warned us, "Don't take any pictures. They are fighting the Republic of South Africa to the south. These guys get real nervous when foreigners come around." I noticed that he accelerated as we passed by. "They know we're missionaries and so far they haven't bothered us, but I like to keep them at a considerable distance."

It was evening by the time we reached Lubango. I realized that I had survived my first day in Angola. Six more to go. Day two wouldn't be so easy.

A DASH IN THE DARK

The next morning, Steve Duncan was anxious to take me to the hospital where he works—200 miles over a countryside littered with blown-up bridges and mined roads. *Another road trip*, I thought. Steve sensed my skepticism, "It'll be okay. A missionary was shot just a few weeks ago, but I think we can make it."

What does he mean "think"? I looked at him like he was crazy. *Doesn't he know? If he's not sure, then why are we even doing this?*

Steve tried to make some phone calls to check out the road conditions and to find out if there had been any reports of rebel activity, but all the phone lines had been cut. He asked some truckers if they knew how safe the trip might be, but nobody could tell us anything. Steve was not easily deterred. He looked over at us, waved his hand, and said, "Let's go."

I learned something about that little phrase from Steve. *Let's go* to him, meant never looking back, always ahead. It also meant that Steve was constantly ready "to go" down the pathway he knew God had prepared for his steps.

We departed about 10:00 A.M. Steve had conveniently forgotten to tell me why it was so crucial that we get an early start. I found out later that if we didn't make it to the hospital before dark, it would be a suicide ride. Soldiers from both sides shoot at anything that moves once night falls.

The morning sun sparkled over the Angolan countryside, displaying its lush savannas. It reminded me of Southern California on a glorious summer day. As the vehicle made its way up into the golden mountains beyond, the terrain became rugged and rocky—much like Arizona. It was by far the most spectacular scenery I had seen in Africa.

I settled back to enjoy the ride, thinking, *This isn't so bad.* I was quickly jolted back into reality when Steve swerved off the road. I flew into the door, then was slung nearly into his lap. I strengthened my grip on the door handle and watched as Steve held a steady speed and then, without flinching, headed right for a ditch.

"What are you doing?" I shouted, but Steve was too busy driving to answer. In full control, he steered toward an embankment. I began to doubt his competence to have a driver's license. Down we went. It seemed like a split second, and before I knew what had really happened, he had maneuvered the vehicle back up on the road. My doubt vanished as he demonstrated his ability to handle the wheel. I was impressed as he geared up and resumed his normal speed.

"What was that all about?" I asked.

Nonchalantly, Steve said, "Oh, a pothole was there a few days ago. Somebody filled it in."

"So? I'm glad someone's repairing the road."

"Road repairs nothin'!" Steve exclaimed. "The guerrillas like to fill potholes with mines."

I fell back into the seat, determined to pray that Steve would miraculously spot every single pothole along the way. After all, our lives depended on it.

The day grew longer. The sun climbed higher. Our clothes became sticky with sweat, and we frequently had to slow down to navigate our way around four- to five-foot craters left by exploded land mines. But we never stopped. It was just too dangerous.

As I squinted from the glaring sun and scanned the countryside, something looked peculiar. I edged up on the seat and pointed to a heap lying beside the road, several hundred feet away.

"What in the world is that?" I asked.

"I don't know," Steve said, "but it wasn't here a few days ago."

We looked with suspicion, trying to figure out what it was. When we got closer, we realized it was an overturned and smoldering semitrailer. We approached the scene carefully and saw that the truck had run over a mine. It was bowed in the middle, a good fifty to a hundred feet off the road. I shuddered to think what kind of powerful land mine could bend and throw an eighteen-wheeler that far. I immediately lost all sense of comfort from that aluminum plate supposedly protecting our own vehicle. *There's no way that a two-inch plate would stop that kind of blast,* I thought. If a mine could lift a semi off the road, it could certainly blow us to the moon.

Delays along the road agitated Steve. When we were more than ready to be there, we were still a long way off. The sun began to fade. So did the smile on Steve's face. We were now looking at the shadows of dusk. I kept remembering Steve's concern about arriving before dark, but it didn't change the fact that the sun was right on schedule—sinking beneath the horizon. Steve's jaw muscles tightened; his grip clenched the wheel. I could sense his cool demeanor growing tense.

"What's the matter?" I asked.

"It's getting dark," Steve answered in a solemn tone, as his eyes surveyed the landscape. "Soldiers will shoot at any headlight pointed in their direction.

"But," he added, "the good news is that we only have twenty miles left."

The same dreadful fear that had been in the pit of my stomach the whole trip seemed to cut right through me. Twenty miles on a U.S. freeway was an easy twenty minutes. Here, we were looking at a good hour or more, and there wasn't nearly that much daylight left. *I'm not gonna make it.* I had managed to keep that fear at bay for most of the day. Now, it was back in full force.

This is one of the few times in my life when I felt I was close to death. Whether the fear was a warning from God or a discouragement from the devil, I don't know. I have faced gunfire many times since that trip but never felt the same haunting dread.

There was any number of ways death could bring us down. The occasional burst of gunfire, Steve's erratic driving, the land mines. For the first time in my life, I realized I could be dead before I even knew I was dying. Here, in the fading shadows of Angola, I could very well be breathing my last few breaths.

Many people have asked, "Are you willing to accept the fact that you put yourself and many of your colleagues at risk? Are you ready for someone to die?" I answer by saying, "God values each human life. I would never act recklessly, but the work to which God has called me takes us to the ditches and gutters of the world—the war and famine zones—where people are in need. The truth is, there is danger in taking risks."

I've heard it said that wherever there is danger, there lurks opportunity. I'd rather live in the face of fear knowing that God will be with me every step of the way than to shrink back and miss an opportunity to serve Him because of all the what-ifs: What if I get shot? What if they turn their backs? What if they don't listen to me? What if the money runs out?

The apostles certainly did not let these questions hinder them—and they didn't travel to the most comfortable places. I don't take anyone with me who doesn't have the same confident passion about serving the Lord in perilous regions around the world. If we want to be used by God, we have no other choice than to trust ourselves to His care and say like Dr. Duncan, "Let's go."

I believe that if we have nothing we're willing to die for, we really have nothing worth living for. But to practice that is a different story. For me, Angola was a test. As the apostle Paul said in Philippians 1:21: "For to me, to live is Christ, and to die is gain."

As thoughts raced through my mind, I watched the sun dip lower. We were kidding ourselves to pretend it was dusk—it was plain ol' dark. But Steve was reluctant to turn the headlights on. When the road eventually disappeared into the blackness of night, he reached over on the dash and with a sigh flicked on the lights.

I suddenly knew what it was like to be on the other side of target practice.

Every inch of the road seemed like a long drawn-out mile as we pondered our fate and envisioned ourselves at the end of a gun barrel. When you're faced with a life-and-death situation, time seems to idle. I am sure that those last few miles weren't nearly as long as they seemed. It was as though we were spinning our wheels but getting nowhere.

After a tense ride, Steve startled me out of deep thought. "There it is!"

"What?" I hollered back unnerved, preparing myself for the worst.

"The lights of the hospital."

I breathed a sigh of relief and leaned up to gaze at the warm glow of the lights in the distance. As the beams glistened brighter, the gates to the remote African hospital came into view. I began to relax as I realized that more than just enemy eyes had watched us along the road: The eyes of Almighty God had been fixed on our vehicle all the way. When I looked into the smiling faces of our welcoming committee, I understood why God's hand had protected us. These dear missionaries and national Christians had been praying for our safety. God had listened and answered.

Steve's strained face broke out into a wide grin. He turned the ignition off and slumped back into the seat. We were dirty, tired, thirsty, hungry, and immensely thankful to be alive. He looked over at me, and said with a little vigor, "Let's go!"

Made it through day two.

Was the risk worth it? No question in my mind. This little mission hospital needed the help of Samaritan's Purse. They needed doctors, medicine, and a truck to haul in supplies. I knew God had led me all this way to help strengthen the arms of those who sacrificially served the Lord in this weary land.

I could have never conveyed the work that was being done in Christ's name to the Samaritan's Purse supporters had I not experienced the joys and sorrows those dear servants of God go through day after day. When we understand the trials that our brothers and sisters endure, it should make us want to reach out and do all that we can to strengthen them so that they can continue serving. *"Each of you should look not only to your own interests, but also to the interests of others"* (Phil. 2:4 NIV).

Isn't this what Christ did for us by coming to this lost and sinful world? God sent His Son to personally experience our cares in this life. Jesus lived like one of us. He suffered. He was tempted. He found out what it was like to be tired, hungry, hunted, betrayed, and ultimately killed. The Bible says, *"Let this mind be in you which was also in Christ Jesus, who . . . made Himself of no reputation, taking the form of a bondservant, and coming in the likeness of men. And being found in appearance as a man, He humbled Himself and became obedient to the point of death, even the death of the cross"* (Phil. 2:5–8). Jesus closely identified with us. He was able to communicate with us, yet He was, and is, the precious Lamb of God who takes away the sins of the world.

This is what my trip to Angola was all about: to help these men and women make the most of their sacrificial living so that they could lead others to Christ. Because the drive was so dangerous, missionaries weren't able to hire trucks at any price to haul goods. The delivery was too risky. Armed with firsthand knowledge of the situation, I was able to explain the needs to our donors and answer their questions and concerns. It gave them an opportunity to help minister to people in Angola by providing for God's servants. As a result, Samaritan's Purse was able to recruit doctors to serve in Angola and to purchase a truck to take shipments of medicine and supplies into the African interior.

One donor, in particular, stands out in my mind. The late Mary Crowley, founder of Home Interiors, Inc. She happened to be a member of my father's board of directors. During a break in a board meeting one day soon after my return, she asked about my trip to Angola. She wanted to know what she could do to help.

When I told her about the need for a special truck to transport medicine and other items to the mission stations, she was a bit skeptical. "But if such a trip is so dangerous to make, what's to keep the truck from being destroyed on its first journey, and risk someone being killed? After all, aren't we trying to save lives?" she asked.

I was prepared for this.

"Mary, I asked the Africans the same question, and they told me, 'Franklin, if Samaritan's Purse buys the truck, that will make it God's truck, and He'll be responsible for what happens to it, right?'" Mary laughed and said, "Good answer." Right then and there, she wrote a check for the entire cost of the vehicle.

Over the years, tons of medicine have been transported in this truck which has now logged over a half million miles. It has survived rolling over many land mines and barely escaped the wrath of gunfire, though it's had a few bullets slam through the windshield and some tires shot out. But, as Dr. Steve Foster told me just recently, "That truck is still serving the Lord." And because of it, needed medicine and supplies have been delivered, enabling doctors like Steve Duncan and Steve Foster to save countless lives. The Lord's hand of protection has guided even that vehicle through perilous times. More important, these faithful physicians were given the greatest opportunity of all: to tell their patients the good news of Jesus Christ.

God used these brave men to teach me about living beyond the limits of fear by trusting the Lord and giving Him room to work, even when the road seems uncertain and is laden with devastating possibilities.

FACING OUR FEARS

Fear of men can knock us out of sync with God. As I look back, I almost allowed fear itself to keep me from Angola. But that small voice within urged me onward. I overcame the first hurdle by stepping inside the aircraft that would take me to Angola. When I arrived, however, fear gripped me once again. Oh, I wasn't afraid that God would forsake me, but I did fear falling prey to men's evil schemes. As I traveled through Angola with Steve Duncan, I saw firsthand how he dealt with fear—he simply put his trust in Almighty God.

If we let fear get the upper hand, it will paralyze us, make us ineffective, and cause us to miss what God has planned for us. In extreme cases, fear can destroy us. *"So we say with confidence, 'The*

Lord is my helper; I will not be afraid. What can man do to me?'" (Heb. 13:6 NIV).

The sad thing is, fear doesn't just consume people in war-torn countries. Fear fills many a pew on Sunday morning. The Holy Spirit may be prompting us to share the gospel with a neighbor or business associate, but the fear that that person will ask a question we can't answer causes us to hold our tongue. What are we to do? Try countering fear with trust.

Jeremiah 1:6–9 says: *"'Ah, Sovereign LORD,' I said, 'I do not know how to speak;' . . . But the LORD said to me, . . . 'You must go to everyone I send you to and say whatever I command you. Do not be afraid of them, for I am with you and will rescue you.' . . . Then the LORD reached out his hand and touched my mouth and said to me, 'Now, I have put my words in your mouth'"* (NIV). This is our promise too: He will put the words in our mouths. We can take courage that God is with us.

Many times fear can be the result of losing our focus. When I first heard the machine-gun fire ripping through the streets below me, I had a choice to make: *Am I going to focus on the threat of men's bullets or on God's sovereign hand of protection?* I had to make a conscious choice to think about God's purpose for seeing me safely to Angola. I knew He had something for me to do.

Fear cannot take hold unless it is fed. Our minds have a tremendous capacity for fantasy. We are able to imagine things that do not even exist. If we dwell on a perceived threat, panic will take over. If we dwell on Christ, peace will prevail. The prophet Isaiah said, *"You will keep him in perfect peace, whose mind is stayed* [focused] *on You, because he trusts in You"* (26:3).

In contrast to fearing men, there is a godly fear. Cromwell said, "Because I fear God, I have no fear of man." Martin Luther agreed: "If there were more fear of God today, there would be less of this licking of men's boots. There are some who go around with their tongues black because they spend so much time licking the boots of men. Why do they do it? There is no fear of God in them. The thing that gives you courage is to fear God." Holy fear keeps us in sync with Him; it actually keeps us fine tuned.

Fear of God means that we owe Him our reverential respect and trust. God promises, *"I will give them singleness of heart and action, so that they will always fear me for their own good and the good of their children after them. . . . I will never stop doing good to them, and I will inspire them to fear me, so that they will never turn away from me"* (Jer. 32:39–40 NIV).

This certainly describes the Christians I met in Angola.

And remember Steve Duncan? He was bound and determined to serve God in Angola. He didn't let the what-ifs limit him. Instead his motto was "Let's go!" and see what God has in store.

That's my reason for living—to share God's gospel—and if that means taking it to dangerous places like Angola, then I have learned to say *let's go* and watch God take us beyond what we could have ever humanly imagined. Those profound little words call to mind Matthew 28:19: *"Go therefore and make disciples of all the nations, baptizing them in the name of the Father and of the Son and of the Holy Spirit."*

K *A-BOOM!* THE GROUND SHOOK. Dennis and I split. Dennis Agajanian is a good friend of mine, and we often travel together. On this occasion Preston Parrish was with us, and we had been touring a refugee camp on the Thai-Cambodian border when a mortar shell exploded not far from us. Dennis and Preston jumped into one ditch; I crashed into another.

I chose the wrong one, and I found myself knee-deep in muck that was crawling with every kind of infectious disease imaginable to man, I'm sure.

In refugee camps, ditches often double as sewers with green slime that skims the surface.

I didn't know which was more hazardous—the crud clinging to me or the shrapnel flying above my head.

"Dennis!" I yelled out. "Where are you?"

"Over here."

I waited for a momentary lull, pulled myself up, and took a couple of huge leaps across the road into the same ditch with Dennis and Preston.

"What happened to you?" Dennis bellowed.

I didn't pay much attention to him. I just hunkered down in the makeshift foxhole. Every now and then we would peer out to see if there was any way of escape. All of a sudden we heard a truck engine crank up. We carefully raised our heads just enough to clear eye level.

Sean Campbell, the project director for the relief work in the camp, was rushing to get the nurses out of the camp clinic for a quick getaway. We thought, *No way is he gonna leave us here.* Ray Charles had a hit song years ago, "Hit the road, Jack, and don't cha come back no mo'." We scrambled out of that filthy ditch and hit the road heading toward Sean's van. We leaped in as Sean put the pedal to the floor, and we had no intention of coming back.

It always amazes me when I hear someone say they think Christians are just naturally weak people. "Christians need a spiritual crutch because they can't make it on their own," they say. After all, the world says, "Wasn't Jesus gentle, loving, kind, and softhearted?" They forget that the same Jesus who invited the little children up onto His lap overthrew the money changers in the temple.

Jesus displayed incredible courage when He willingly took on the sins of all mankind—the lies, murders, robberies, rapes, and all the other evils. When you talk about courage, you have to talk about the cross. Jesus was beaten, cursed, spat on, and stripped. He suffered every indignity imaginable. With one whisper, He could have brought an immediate end to His pain. But Jesus was the toughest man who ever lived. He endured. He stayed with God's plan. He went to the cross because He loved you and me. He knew that was the only way we could come into God's presence.

It takes courage to keep in sync with God. It takes grit to be an ambassador for Christ and go beyond the limits to carry out His will. Yes, Christianity is about being kind, considerate, compassionate, and loving. But there's also a bold side to our faith.

Dennis Agajanian is a living example of this. About six feet four, with the girth to support it, Dennis looks like he could be Hulk Hogan's tag-team partner in WrestleMania. But he makes his living on the neck of a guitar. His fingers can fly, especially when he's playing bluegrass. Johnny Cash has called him the "fastest flat-pick guitarist in the world."

Whenever I'm traveling overseas, I like to take Dennis with me. He's a rugged man, quick thinking, and if I'm in danger, he's the type of person I want to have around. I think either one of us would take a bullet for the other if it came down to that.

But you don't have to go overseas to display courage. Dennis exhibited inspiring courage in the Colorado mountains. He wasn't facing an opposing army; he simply had to stand up to a Christian who was out of sync with God. That can take more guts than facing mortar bombs.

YOU CALL YOURSELF A CHRISTIAN?

For the past fifteen years, Dennis and I have participated in a charity event known as the Colorado 500, a motorcycle charity ride that supports local hospitals and schools. It can sometimes appear to be the who's who of the racing world, with some of the most famous drivers in the world participating. At least 300 dirt bikes cross a single-track trail through narrow mountain passes and over the rugged Colorado terrain.

The day before the ride, Dennis and I were adjusting the fuel/air mixtures in our carburetors to prepare them for high altitude. We were trying to hurry so that we could test-ride our bikes later that day.

A man and woman had pulled a white trailer up next to where we were working. The woman was one of those bubbly, vivacious types—overly friendly. She was an attractive lady with sandy hair and blue eyes. As Dennis and I fine-tuned our bikes, she came down the steps of the RV and introduced herself. In the course of the conversation, she mentioned that she was a Christian. She hung around for a while asking a lot of questions.

Her actions made me a little nervous, so I excused myself.

"Dennis, I'll be back in a couple of hours. We'll test the bikes then." I headed to the Aspen Airport to meet a friend and fellow motorcycle rider, Pete Robinson.

When I got back to the ranch, I found Dennis's face red and the woman's eyes bloodshot. The man who was with the young woman didn't look too happy either. In fact, he looked like he wanted to kill someone. I approached with a bit of caution.

"Dennis," I pulled him aside, "I've only been gone an hour and a half, and it looks like you've got everybody hoppin' mad about something. What's goin' on?"

"That woman," Dennis answered pointing, "told me she's heard me play and loves my music. She's been hanging around ever since you left."

"Say what?" I looked at him puzzled. "Why is that a problem?"

Dennis told me what had transpired after I had left. The guy she was staying with had stepped out of the trailer. He was much older. She quickly introduced him to Dennis, but Dennis began to sense their relationship wasn't what it ought to be. Maybe it was the guilty look on the guy's face.

"Is this your husband?" Dennis quizzed.

"No."

"Okay," Dennis paused. "Who is he?"

"My boyfriend."

"Boyfriend?"

"Mmmhmm."

"And this is your camper here?"

"No, it's his."

"His, huh? So are you driving back to Denver tonight?"

"No."

"You're going to stay with him?"

"Yeah."

"And you call yourself a Christian?"

"Well, sure."

Dennis had looked this girl straight in the eyes and said, "Don't you know this is wrong? This is a sin against God. Don't do this."

The woman stuttered. Dennis didn't let up. "God loves you. You can't stay with him. It's sin and you know it."

She had finally turned away in tears. Dennis didn't know what to do. He can't stand to see a girl cry. He bent down to check the air pressure in his bike's tires. When he looked over his shoulder she was still crying.

Dennis had said with a hint of compassion, "In spite of what you do, God loves you and wants to forgive you. When you look into your boyfriend's eyes tonight, remember that you are hurting the heart of God."

That's when I pulled up.

After hearing Dennis's story, I couldn't help but admire his honesty and, yes, his fearlessness. Dennis had confronted this young woman head-on. He didn't enjoy doing it; in fact, he was rather uneasy about the whole incident, but he believed (and rightly so) that if she wanted to call herself a Christian and a follower of Jesus Christ, then she ought to live like one by obeying God's Word, which says, *"Get rid of all moral filth and the evil that is so prevalent and humbly accept the word planted in you"* (James 1:21 NIV).

The next day, Wally Dallenbach, the host for this charity event, and his wife, Peppy, asked Dennis to play a few songs and me to say a few words and pray before the ride got started. After Dennis sang, he stood at the back of the crowd. He noticed the young woman there. Dennis doesn't do well disguising his feelings. What you see is what you get. He can't pull the shade on sin and pretend it isn't there.

The woman discreetly eyed Dennis with a somewhat forlorn look. Dennis stared back, determined to give the Holy Spirit a little help. He pointed to her and mouthed the words *God loves you.*

She started to cry. The boyfriend glared back at Dennis with malice. He was well aware of what was going on, but a man his age and size was no match for Dennis, so he had no choice but to keep his distance.

After I finished praying, all the guys headed for their bikes and began putting on their gear. Three hundred dirt bikes revved up in unison and spewed their exhaust into the air. The noise was deafening, like a million hornets surrounded us.

Within seconds, the Colorado 500 was underway and our concentration was refocused on keeping our wheels on course.

I never saw that woman again, but Dennis did.

BOLD LIVING

What I appreciate about Dennis is that he didn't allow a woman's flattery to influence his convictions. Some people might think Dennis should have been less direct, but our fear of offending others can have grave eternal consequences.

The fact is, if we want to make a difference in the kingdom of God, at times we must act with uncompromising boldness and live it as well. As an evangelist, I preach openly against sin—and that's not too fashionable these days. Many would argue that it simply isn't politically correct, but God says in Ezekiel:

> I have made you a watchman . . . ; therefore you shall hear a word from My mouth and warn them for Me. When I say to the wicked, "O wicked man, you shall surely die!" and you do not speak to warn the wicked from his way, that wicked man shall die in his iniquity; but his blood I will require at your hand. (33:7–8)

Dennis confronted this woman in the footsteps of the Old Testament prophet Ezekiel, whose name means "strengthened by God."

Dennis didn't let his fan's admiration or the boyfriend's angry reaction deter him from speaking out against sin. Dennis simply spoke the truth, and the truth, as we'll see, eventually set that woman free.

FEELING GOOD

Our reluctance to confront others can be our mistaken belief that we as Christians should simply make people feel good. Nowhere does the Bible say we're to feel good about sin.

Imagine if while building the ark Noah had simply said, "Hey, you down there, I want you to know you're going to get a little wet. Please, don't panic. It's nothing to get anxious or uncomfortable about, but you need to think about getting an umbrella."

Each person we meet on a daily basis who does not know Christ is hell bound. That may make some folks bristle—but it's a fact. When we refuse to warn people that their actions and lifestyles have eternal consequences, we're not doing them any favors. If everybody feels good about his or her sin, why would anyone repent?

I have heard it said that we want a God without wrath, who took man without sin, into a kingdom without justice, through the ministrations of a Christ without a cross.

The truth is, judgment is coming. There is a heaven and there is a hell. In our human weakness we want to say, "Oh, we love you, we accept you just as you are. We understand why you live the way you live. You don't need to change. You just need to know that God loves you and understands you in spite of your special problems."

That is *not* the gospel message.

The *gospel* literally means "good news." Who doesn't want to hear good news? Surprisingly, more people than you might think. Our society rushes to the newsstand to buy the latest sensational headline about someone wallowing in sinful behavior. People actually pay good money to read this stuff. But we have a responsibility to tell them that God offers freedom from the muck and mire the world advertises and sells.

The apostle Paul clearly states,

> *Now, brothers, I want to remind you of the gospel I preached to you, which you received and on which you have taken your stand. By this gospel you are saved, if you hold firmly to the word I preached to you. Otherwise, you have believed in vain. For what I received I passed on to you as of first importance: that Christ died for our sins according to the Scriptures, that he was buried, that he was raised on the third day according to the Scriptures.* (1 Cor. 15:1–4 NIV)

God is a righteous God, a jealous God, a consuming God. But here is some good news: God is also compassionate.

Jesus, in Mark 1, demonstrates this when a man with leprosy (symbolic of sin) came to him one day and entreated the Lord to make him clean. *"Filled with compassion, Jesus reached out his hand and touched the man. . . . Immediately . . . he was cured"* (vv. 41–42 NIV).

Dennis didn't have the power to forgive this young woman of her sin, but he knew who did. He wanted to point her to the Savior, and that's what all Christians should do when a sinner or floundering saint stumbles across our pathway—reach out in compassion. If we're willing to confess our sins, repent of our sins, and receive His Son, Jesus Christ, as our Lord and Savior, He is willing to forgive us and save us *from* our sins. And in the case of a Christian who has lost the way, God will restore him. That's mighty good news.

Some churches make the mistake of preaching only fire and brimstone. That's not God's full message, either. God is eager to forgive us, provided we approach Him through His Son, Jesus Christ.

For God did not send his Son into the world to condemn the world, but to save the world through him. Whoever believes in him is not condemned, but whoever does not believe stands condemned already because he has not believed in the name of God's one and only Son. (John 3:17–18 NIV)

Put to death, therefore, whatever belongs to your earthly nature: sexual immorality, impurity, lust, evil desires and greed, which is idolatry. Because of these, the wrath of God is coming. (Col. 3:5–6 NIV)

When we speak the truth to our friends and loved ones, let's remember to do it in love as the Bible commands. *"Brothers* [and sisters], *if someone is caught in a sin, you who are spiritual should restore him gently"* (Gal. 6:1 NIV). As believers it is our duty to be obedient.

Do You Remember Me?

About two years after Dennis confronted the young woman at the Colorado 500, he was playing at a church in Denver. After the concert, a woman came up to him and asked, "Do you remember me?"

"No, I'm sorry I don't," Dennis confessed.

"Two years ago, I was at the Colorado 500, living in sin with a man, and you rebuked me. Remember?"

Dennis swallowed hard, ready for a confrontation.

"I was afraid to give up my relationship for fear of being alone," the woman continued, much to Dennis's surprise. "I went home after the event and asked God to forgive me. I want you to know that today I'm happily married and a new mother. You cared enough to speak the truth, not just what I wanted to hear. Thank you for helping me get my life right with the Lord. I couldn't be happier."

When Dennis and I return each year for the Colorado 500, we think of that young lady and rejoice that her life is changed. To live a life beyond the limits, we must learn to be courageous when dealing with those who are steeped in worldly lifestyles. Once we're fine-tuned this way, there are *no limits* to how God can use us. This is a promise: *"Be strong and very courageous. Be careful to obey all the law . . . do not turn from it to the right or to the left, that you may be successful wherever you go"* (Josh. 1:7 NIV).

MAMA GUMP

W HAT WOULD LIFE BE without encountering characters now and then, those colorful people who make lasting impressions and give new meaning to the distinctive word *individual?* Conformity is comfortable ground for most. But I seem to be attracted to unique personalities—men and women who are not afraid just to be themselves. Dennis Agajanian would definitely fit into the category of rugged individuals—he stands up for what he believes no matter what. In fact, I would go further to say that he's in a league all by himself!

I got the shock of my life a few years ago when I met a little mountain woman—someone I would have guessed to be timid, maybe even afraid of her own very small shadow. She may be petite in stature, especially standing next to Dennis Agajanian, but she is every bit his match in fearless conviction. With her there are no masks.

I'll never forget the Friday after Thanksgiving, 1994. I was glad to be home with my family for the long holiday weekend, away from the flurry of a busy office.

The late autumn air was filled with the smell of wood burning through the hollers. A gentle wind blew the brilliant maple leaves to the ground and swirled them around my ankles. I was out in back of the house chopping a supply of firewood for the winter and trying to burn the extra pounds I had put on from the day before.

My workout came to an abrupt end when one of my boys ran out to tell me I had a call. I was relishing the peacefulness of the outdoors and didn't care much about talking on the phone. So I shrugged the message off. But when I looked toward the house, Jane Austin was standing at the door. "Phone call, Franklin. I think you better take it."

I grumbled a little as I leaned the ax up against the woodpile, brushed the sawdust off my hands, and headed to the kitchen. My office was technically closed, but because we were entering our busiest season, we had someone on duty to answer the phones.

When I picked up the receiver, my receptionist said, "Mr. Graham?"

"Yes, Ma'am."

"There's a woman out in the parking lot with some shoe boxes for you."

I told her that I was busy at home and suggested that the woman leave the boxes at the office.

"Mr. Graham, I really think you should come and meet her."

Our receptionist had worked with me for many years. I knew she wouldn't insist if it didn't seem important.

I sighed and then told her I would be right there. I climbed into the pickup and traveled the short distance down a gravel road to my office.

Shoe boxes have a lot to do with why this is our busiest time of year. Since 1993, Samaritan's Purse has worked through families, churches, and schools in many countries around the world to collect shoe boxes filled with Christmas gifts. They are packed primarily by children in Western countries for needy children around the world. The program is called Operation Christmas Child.

The idea is to take an empty shoe box and fill it with toys, school supplies, candy, maybe some warm mittens, for either a boy or a girl, and send it to Samaritan's Purse along with five dollars to help ship the boxes overseas. Then we take them to children all over the world. The joy and excitement the gifts bring to kids of all ages is indescribable.

The first year we did this, we expected to receive a few thousand boxes. Instead, over twenty thousand poured into our Boone office. Operation Christmas Child took off like a rocket and spread like wildfire. It kindled passionate generosity in people's hearts. The idea of kids giving to kids electrifies a family—the family gets a church excited—and before we know it, entire communities join our efforts. Whether rich or poor, filling a shoe box is a realistic goal for anyone to reach—and the results are dynamite.

What excited me about the concept in the beginning was the outreach for the gospel. After all, each shoe box represents one child, and each child represents one precious soul. Bob Pierce always used to say, "Buddy, I can't help everybody, but I can help some." Operation Christmas Child is a one-on-one ministry—one child giving to another and one family reaching out to another family, distributing gifts from one city or community at a time.

Our little logo is a shoe box with airplane wings on it—or, as I like to think of them, angel wings that carry the good news of Jesus Christ right into the hands and hearts of the little children. So actually, these shoe boxes are vehicles for the Christmas story. That's exactly what the gospel is—Jesus Christ coming down to earth to offer us His great forgiveness, acceptance, and love.

In a world where life for many children is harsh and cruel, what do you think a child will do when he or she receives a box filled with toys and candy—a small present by American standards but unbelievably generous by their own? Most often, a child will unwrap the shoe box, take out just one piece of candy or one small gift, and hand the box back. When we tell them, "No, the whole thing is yours," their little eyes peer back into the box in disbelief—some cry, others giggle, most just hug the box close to their grateful hearts.

With thoughts of the project filling my mind, I pulled into the parking lot. Shoe boxes come in all year, but people delivering them to our office between Thanksgiving and Christmas is a daily occurrence. Why should this be treated as some special delivery? I parked my truck behind a bigger one with a West Virginia license plate on the back. *Surely*, I thought, *she didn't drive all the way down here today.*

I walked inside the lobby, figuring the whole visit wouldn't take longer than five minutes. The receptionist pointed toward the family looking at pictures in the hallway. The little lady couldn't have weighed ninety pounds, soaking wet. I walked over and introduced myself. She had an infectious smile and a spark that caught my eye.

"Brother Graham," she said, "I'm Mary. Gotcha some shoe boxes fer God. Where do you want 'em?"

"Well, thank you, Mary" I said. "Why don't you just leave them here in the foyer? We'll stack them up against the wall."

"I gotcha twelve hundred."

My eyes bulged. "Twelve hundred? Well, my goodness. Don't leave them here! Let's take them to the warehouse."

Sure enough, she had driven to Boone that day in a thirty-foot, twenty-ton panel truck. Her son, a stocky young man, hopped in the cab and backed that truck up to the loading dock. The family began pulling boxes from the truck faster than I could count them. They would toss several down to me, and I would stack them inside the warehouse. Watching Mary's enthusiasm made me feel like I was helping Santa unload his sleigh.

I was deeply impressed by this little mountain woman. How did she gather so many gifts? Where could anyone find that many empty shoe boxes in the first place? I watched her direct traffic as her family bounced in and out of that truck. I thought, *This lady has something special! Maybe I should invite her to go with us to Bosnia in a couple of weeks. Bet she could help put these shoe boxes in the right hands.* I initially dismissed the thought, figuring she had never heard of Bosnia. Besides, she might be insulted if I invited her to go into a war zone.

Still, I have always been the impulsive type. I don't know how the Lord speaks to other people, but He frequently speaks to me through a strong impression that moves my heart. This one was really thumping.

"Mary, how did you hear about this project?" I asked.

"I was watchin' the television and saw you talk on Brother Paul and Sister Jan's show. Didn't catch the whole thing, but you said you needed shoe boxes fer God, so I went out and gotcha some."

"But how'd you get twelve hundred?"

Her son grinned proudly as she told me the story. "I went up and down the hollers, tellin' everybody that Brother Graham needed shoe boxes fer God. I went to the churches and told them Brother Graham needed boxes filled with gifts fer the chillun in Boze-ne-a. The chillun need help, and Brother Graham wants to give 'em shoe boxes.

"And, Brother Graham, I gotcha some, didn't I?"

"Bless your heart, Mary, you sure did."

I stood there not believing what I was hearing or seeing. Who would expect a poor little lady who hardly had a dime to her name to go out into impoverished coal mine surroundings to collect gifts for the poor people in Bosnia? I was impressed that she didn't let herself be limited by her own need. Instead, she spent her time challenging neighbors to give, trusting the Lord. That year she collected more boxes for children in Bosnia than any other single individual. Her accomplishment was doubly impressive in that she had not collected these shoe boxes from the wealthy suburbs of Chicago, Boston, or Seattle—she had assembled them from people scattered through the mountain hollers of West Virginia who were living in poverty themselves. It reminded me of the apostle Paul's comments about the Christians in Macedonia who gave sacrificially, contributing their resources for others:

Out of the most severe trial, their overflowing joy and their extreme poverty welled up in rich generosity. For I testify that they gave as much as they were able, and even beyond their ability. Entirely on their own, they urgently pleaded with us for the privilege of sharing in this service to the saints. And they did not do as we expected, but they gave themselves first to the Lord and then to us in keeping with God's will. (2 Cor. 8:2–5 NIV)

I couldn't brush the impulse away. I took a deep breath and said, "Mary, how would you like to go with us to Bosnia to help give these boxes away?"

"I'll go."

She answered so quickly that I wasn't sure she understood what I was asking; did she realize what kind of place I was talking about? Maybe she didn't know that the country was embroiled in a nasty civil war.

"Ever been to Bosnia?" I asked.

"Nope."

"Ever been overseas?"

"Nope."

"You know, they're shootin' over there. There's a war going on. Got a bulletproof vest?"

"What fer? I got the Holy Spirit of God, young man." She waved her hand in the air. "I have angels that surround me and watch over and protect me." Her eyes got real big, as if she could see the angels in the air. The tone in her voice picked up the rhythm of an old-time gospel preacher.

I smiled at her depth of faith. She was some kind of woman. "Believe me, Mary," I said, "you'll be just fine."

I called Ross Rhoads, one of my closest friends and a member of our board of directors who was responsible for leading our team to Bosnia that year. "Ross, I have invited a little mountain woman from West Virginia to accompany the team this year." I wanted him to know that this was not just a little lady from the hills. "This is a powerful woman unlike any you have ever met.

"Ross, this lady can make things happen!" I told him.

"I look forward to meeting her. Carol [his wife] and I will be sure she is well cared for."

And they did. Mary went to Bosnia with us days later with no protest from her family whatsoever.

On Christmas Eve, shortly after he arrived home from Bosnia, I called Ross again. "How did our friend from West Virginia do?"

Ross couldn't find enough words of praise. With the graciousness he's known for, he said, "Oh, she was such a blessing. She put her arms around those kids, she prayed with them, she cried with them, she touched them. At times, she even acted like one of them! And they loved her. The Bosnian people were surprised that she would put aside her own problems and come all the way to Bosnia to help them.

"Her presence was really something special," he added, "not just for them, but for all of us on the team."

FROM THE POOR HOUSE TO THE WHITE HOUSE

Who is this woman? The people from her neck of the woods in Ikes Fork call her Mury [Mary] Damron.

The Christmas of 1995 will always be memorable. Mary helped to collect not just twelve hundred shoe boxes, but over six thousand. She had a mountain of them. Mary was fast becoming a bit of a local celebrity. Because of her travels throughout the region campaigning for shoe boxes, she was written up in a local West Virginia newspaper. Who would ever think that somebody in the White House would get hold of a small article from the hills?

It so happened that the President was planning to send troops to Bosnia to help implement the Dayton Peace Accord, which was scheduled to be signed in France the day after an upcoming news conference. He wanted to showcase several civilians who had already been involved in Bosnia through volunteer efforts. They scanned the Internet and stumbled across the write-up about Mary. She was a perfect fit.

One afternoon in early December, Mary answered the phone and got the shock of her life.

"Is this Mary Damron?" the caller asked.

"Yep," Mary said.

"This is the White House."

"No, it ain't."

"Yes, it is."

"No, it ain't."

There was a long pause. "I'm calling on behalf of the President."

"No, you ain't."

Mary couldn't believe that the White House would call her, and it took some convincing before she would accept the fact that it was true. Once she realized that somebody really was calling on behalf of the President, she quietly took down the information, still in disbelief. Not long after her conversation ended, my telephone rang.

"Brother Graham," she said, "the Prez-i-dent wants me up there in Washington."

"That's wonderful, Mary," I replied.

"I don't feel comfortable going to Washington."

"Well, Mary," I said, "that doesn't matter. He's the President, and if he calls you to the White House, you should go."

"Brother Graham, I've never been there. I'm just a poor country girl, a mountain woman. I'm not sure I'd fit in."

There was a long pause. "How 'bout if you go with me?" she asked.

"Mary, he hasn't invited me," I protested.

"If you cain't go, I ain't goin'," Mary said.

I knew that Mary could not decline such an invitation. I agreed to call the White House and try to get it all worked out.

When I called the President's social liaison and explained Mary's hesitation to come without me, the lady politely said, "But, Mr. Graham, the President hasn't invited you."

"I realize that," I said, "but Mary is uneasy about coming. She'll feel much better if I come with her."

"You wouldn't be able to attend the sessions," the aide asserted. "You'd have to sit out in the hall."

"That won't bother me," I said. "I spent half my school years sitting in the hall."

The White House agreed that I could accompany Mary and her family, and a few days later I left Boone for Washington.

That's My Mama Up There

I had promised that I would fly into Bluefield, West Virginia—the nearest airport to Ikes Fork—to meet Mary, her husband, and her two children. As I taxied to a stop in front of the small terminal, I saw them waiting anxiously. They had their duffel bags packed and were ready for their visit to the nation's capital. Or were they?

I climbed out of the plane and walked over to meet them.

Television cameras greeted my arrival into Bluefield. This was a big headline in the Appalachian hills—COAL MINER'S WIFE TO MEET PRESIDENT OF THE UNITED STATES. From the hollers of West Virginia to 1600 Pennsylvania Avenue!

After a few interviews, I boarded the Damron family into the Mitsubishi, and filed my flight plan to Dulles Airport. I had requested a van to meet us upon arrival and take us into the heart of the city. When we touched down and unloaded the luggage, a stretch limousine pulled up alongside the plane. I tried to explain to the driver that a mistake had been made. "We are supposed to have a van take us into D.C.," I insisted.

"Mr. Graham," the driver said, "all we have available right now are limos, but we'll only charge you the van rate."

It wasn't the cost I was concerned about as much as it was the image. But the driver convinced me that if we were going to get downtown on time, we'd have to take the limousine, so all five of us piled into the polished black stretch limo. Mary's two children thought they had died and gone to heaven.

"Mama!" her ten-year-old daughter, Ashleigh, exclaimed. "They got a bar! In a car!"

"Don't touch that," Mary whispered, pushing the little girl's hand away.

"And peanuts!" her son added.

"Don't eat those," Mary scolded.

But they just couldn't resist them. The sunroof fascinated them, but they had the most fun with the electric button that controlled the glass between the passengers and the chauffeur. "Y'all keep your hands off all these fancy gadgets," Mary insisted. They were so caught up in pushing buttons and switching dials that they paid little attention to their mother's chiding or the monuments and historical buildings along the way. It was an entirely new world to them, and I have to admit, I got a kick out of watching their eyes snap. I am sure the driver had to wonder who had come to town.

"You know, Mama," Mary's son said with a slow drawl as he fiddled with the backseat control panel, "You saw Brother Graham on the TV, went out and got some shoe boxes, took 'em down thar to Carolina, you got sent off to Boze-ne-a, and now the Prez-i-dent's done called you to Washin'ton. You're nothin' but a Mama Gump."

With that, I lost it. I couldn't help but laugh—and so did Mary. He was referring, of course, to the novel and movie *Forrest Gump*, in which a country boy (portrayed in the movie by Tom Hanks) from Greenbow, Alabama, stumbles onto one momentous thing after another throughout life and ends up meeting the President.

After a rather entertaining ride to D.C., we arrived at the hotel in time to meet with representatives from the White House. They were coming to introduce themselves to Mary and to double-check her story so that the President could be fully and accurately briefed. The President's aides were a little uncomfortable about talking with Mary. But they questioned her extensively about her volunteer service, and she chatted away like she had known them her whole life. By the end of the interview, Mary had disarmed them, and they left that night completely at ease, and quite impressed with this little woman from the mountains of West Virginia.

Before Mary and her family went back to their room, I carefully suggested, "Mary, since you are here to tell about your work with the shoe boxes, why don't you all wear our Operation Christmas Child sweatshirts tomorrow?" I had a brand-new one for each member of the family.

She grinned and without hesitation said, "Well, sure, we'll put 'em on, Brother Graham."

The next morning we were up early. The Damron family met me in the hotel lobby, and they were proudly wearing the shirts I had given to them. The limo pulled up to the door right on time. Being just a stone's throw from the White House, there wasn't much time to talk, but Mary asked, "Brother Graham, I've been wonderin'—do you think I should pray fer the Prez-i-dent? Do you think he'd mind if I prayed fer him in that there Oval Office?"

I was touched by her sensitivity. At the same time I was amazed by her boldness.

"No, Mary, I don't think he'd mind," I said.

We had been instructed by the President's liaison to enter through the White House Guard Gate off Pennsylvania Avenue. We were taken as far as the car was allowed to travel, and the driver let us out at the designated gate.

After receiving clearance from White House security, we were all ushered into the hall outside the Oval Office. Within minutes,

Mary was taken in to meet with the President. But I didn't have to sit out in the hall all by myself; Mary's husband and two kids waited there with me. Forty minutes later an aide appeared and escorted us into the Roosevelt Room, across from the Oval Office. We were told that the President would conduct his scheduled press conference soon. With him would be five volunteers who the President felt had made a significant contribution to the people of Bosnia, among them Mama Gump.

As we waited for the President's entrance, an aide walked up, tapped me on the shoulder, and said, "Mr. Graham, the President would like to see you."

The President and I had met before in the aftermath of the Oklahoma City bombing. I had joined my mother and father, along with the President and Mrs. Clinton, in a private meeting with the family members of Secret Service personnel who had been killed in the tragic blast.

I was led into the Oval Office. The President, standing alone, greeted me with an extended hand and great big grin. "Franklin, how are you? How's your mom and dad?"

"We're all fine, thank you, sir."

The President folded his arms and cut right to business, "Now, Franklin, that woman from West Virginia, where did you find her?"

I thought, *Oh, no. What has Mary done? What did she say to him?* Before I could respond, the President continued, "I can tell you right now, she is some kind of woman. Where is she from in West Virginia?"

"Some holler called Ikes Fork—I think."

"I don't believe I have ever met anybody quite like her."

Our conversation was about to end as I saw some senators walk in, obviously needing the President's attention. An aide started to lead me out, but the President grabbed my arm and said, "No, Franklin, I'd like you to stay." To my surprise, he dismissed the senators, and questioned me further.

"Is Mary on your payroll?" he asked.

"No, sir, she's not."

"Well, she ought to be. She's the most powerful woman I've ever met. If I had five women like her, I could take Congress." I pondered that for a moment.

After we exchanged a few more comments, I was taken back to be seated for the press conference. Mary's son, Tad, was with his daddy and little sister in the row behind me. Tad was as proud as could be of his mama. I noticed he was holding a video camera that he had borrowed to capture this historic event in his mama's life. He wasn't trying to be conspicuous, but with his jeans, dark goatee, and mustache, he was drawing some attention as he kept raising up from the chair trying to catch the first glimpse of his mother walking in with the President. My heart began to pump a little faster when a Secret Service agent leaned over me from the aisle and pulled Tad's sleeve. In a rather commanding tone, he said, "Young man, you're going to have to put that camera away."

Tad didn't blink. He didn't lower his voice, either. "My mama's gonna be up there, and I wanna take a picture of my mama."

The agent was an imposing figure with one of those immaculate power suits hanging from his six-foot frame. This guy wasn't fooling around. He was used to getting his way—on the spot. "You are not authorized to take pictures. Put your camera down," he ordered.

"This is the most important day of my mama's life, and I'm gonna take a picture of her with the Prez-i-dent. All these other people got cameras, so why cain't I have one?"

"No, all these others do not have cameras," the Secret Service agent insisted.

"How 'bout them?" Tad jerked his thumb toward the wall of journalists standing in the back, with about a dozen video cameras and twice as many still photographers.

I've never seen a Secret Service agent get so flustered. I rubbed my hand over my forehead and wondered how long Tad would keep it up. The President was about to walk into the room, and that agent sure didn't want a scene. It was evident, though, that he had never met anybody quite like Tad.

I tried to distance myself, but the agent kept looking at me, assuming we were together. I was taken back by his tolerance. This powerhouse could have removed Tad from the room without explanation. But he drew a deep breath and said, "You are an invited guest. You should respect the regulations. You do not have the right to take a picture." He pointed to the back of the room, "They are the press, and they're authorized. You are not authorized."

"Well, that's my mama up there, and I don't see why I cain't take a picture if everybody else can take a picture."

I realized this standoff could go south on me real quick, so I leaned over and said, "Tad, just put the camera down for a minute."

With some reluctance, he did so, and the agent nodded with thanks for my intervention. After he disappeared into the packed room, I turned to Tad and whispered, "When your mama and the President walk in, lift the camera up and roll the tape, then put it right back down. The agent won't want to make a scene then. No one will dare walk over and take it away from you while the President is giving his address."

That seemed to satisfy him, but he stayed on the edge of his seat with his hands positioned, ready to capture his mama's first live news conference. The Secret Service agent seemed to fade from the scene—but "Mury" made her debut that day, and Tad has the tape to prove it.

"Can I Pray fer You?"

Mary's family beamed as she walked out with the President and First Lady. After delivering a short speech detailing his plan for sending troops into Bosnia, the President introduced the volunteers whom he had chosen to spotlight that morning. He introduced Mary as a true "individual" whose work with Samaritan's Purse had impacted multitudes of children in the former Yugoslav republic. He spent the majority of time emphasizing Mary's quest—collecting thousands of shoe boxes from the poor children in West Virginia to be given to the more needy children in Bosnia. He didn't shy away from praising Mary for her hard and dedicated work.

Following the news conference, a member of the presidential staff called Mary's family and me into the Oval Office for pictures. I looked around to make sure that Tad's camera was safely packed in his duffel bag. When I walked through the door and spotted Mary, I noticed that she was stooped over her blue canvas travel bag she had been holding.

I thought, *Oh boy, what has she got in there?*

"Mr. Prez-i-dent," she raised up, "I got somethin' fer you."

I was embarrassed when she handed him a copy of a children's book I had written, *Miracle in a Shoebox*, a story about Operation Christmas Child, and how a family in the United States packed shoe boxes for children living in Bosnia during the height of the war. It wasn't exactly a book that would win a literary prize. *Please, Mary, don't give that to him*, I pleaded silently.

But before I could make eye contact with her, the President said, "Thank you, Mary. I look forward to reading that."

I'll bet, I thought to myself. *No way are you going to read that thing.*

Then Mary pulled out another copy. "Mrs. Prez-i-dent," she began—and I thought, *Mrs. President? Now Mary's become a prophet!* "I got one fer you too."

"Thank you, Mary," the First Lady said. "I'll share this with Chelsea."

Then Mary reached a third time into her bag.

I swallowed hard and wondered, *What now?*

My heart melted when she pulled out one of the empty shoe

boxes that had been specially printed for Operation Christmas Child by Jim Hodges of the Royal Paper Box Company in California.

"Mr. Prez-i-dent, will you fill this one fer me?"

The President seemed truly surprised by Mary's modest request. "Mary," he said, "I'll be glad to fill a shoe box for you."

When the President stretched out his hands to receive the box, Mary, as bold as a lion and as gentle as a dove, said, "Mr. Prez-i-dent, do you car if I pray fer you?"

In that fleeting moment, the President became solemn. A little mountain woman took him completely off guard, but he graciously agreed. "I would appreciate that, Mary. Thank you."

Mary took the lead in joining our hands and then prayed a short prayer: "Our heavenly Father, we pray fer the Prez-i-dent and all the responsibilities that he has to shoulder. We pray that You would guide and direct him as he makes decisions that affect all our lives. We pray You would watch o'r him and protect him and give him strength fer this day. In Christ's name we pray. Amen."

When I opened my eyes, the President seemed moved. Maybe he could sense that this woman's power within was God's strength from above. There's no question that on that day in the Oval Office, Mary made a lasting impression with the commander in chief. After all, our brief five-minute photo session with the President of the United States turned into a twenty-five minute chat instead, ending with a little prayer meeting with the King of kings. In one twenty-four hour period, God brought Mary from the poor house to the White House. Talk about living beyond the limits!

It was a demonstration of the truth Paul expressed to the Corinthians:

> *Brothers, think of what you were when you were called.*
> *Not many of you were wise by human standards; not many*
> *were influential; not many were of noble birth. But God*

chose the foolish things of the world to shame the wise; God chose the weak things of the world to shame the strong. He chose the lowly things of this world and the despised things—and the things that are not—to nullify the things that are, so that no one may boast before him. (1 Cor. 1:26–29 NIV)

A few days later, our team left for Bosnia—armed with Mary Damron and a special shoe box packed by the First Family. I told Mary that we wanted to be sure and give the presidential shoe box to an extraordinary child. When we arrived in Bosnia, the search began. We had several distribution programs throughout the cities and villages, but when we arrived in the town of Bihác, we found just the right little girl.

Bihác had been in the news quite a bit. The enemy had surrounded the area for three years, and Bihác had endured daily assaults with mortar shells. It's still hard to fathom that anyone could have survived the constant bombardment. Those who did suffered through it with severe injuries.

One victim who was brought to our attention was little Zlada Dich—she had been in the wrong place at the wrong time. A mortar bomb had exploded, shattering one of her legs. When local workers told us about Zlada, our hearts were moved to learn that in spite of the great pain and terror she endured, she never shed a tear. During her stay in the hospital, the doctors amputated her injured leg. She hobbled down the halls on her crutches, bringing cheer and encouragement to other amputees. Zlada was chosen to receive the presidential box. And who better to make the presentation than Mary? The very shoe box that she had handed to the President to fill, Mary now handed to the little girl to empty. And all of our hearts overflowed that day.

Watching Mary in Bosnia was a real lesson in compassion for me. As we wandered through the hospital ward in Bihác, I came across a very sick little boy. I picked up a box and put it in bed next to him, but he showed no response. I opened the package and tipped it slightly so he could see what was inside. He wouldn't even smile. I tried to get him to play with one of the cars, but he just wasn't interested. I started looking around for some help. One of the nurses came over and in broken English explained that the little boy had been there for several months. He had witnessed the murder of his parents and hadn't responded to anyone since that day. I'm sure the nurse thought I was offended that the boy didn't show any interest, but that wasn't the case; my heart broke for him. I just couldn't walk away without making some kind of connection.

I looked around the room and saw Mary playing with a group of kids. Dennis Agajanian and Ricky Skaggs, who were with me, were like troubadours of goodwill, roaming from ward to ward playing their guitars as the children watched with delight. I hollered above the music and commotion, "Mary!"

She looked up as I motioned for her to join me.

"I've got a special child for you," I said.

With one big sweep, Mary hugged the group of little ones she had been playing with and was over to the bed railing in a flash. "Mary," I said, "he just needs a little love."

Gently pushing me aside, she said, "Well, then, let me love on him for a little bit."

Mary leaned over the metal bar and started unpacking the box of toys, but the boy's expression didn't change. Mary began lightly poking him in ribs and tickling him as she teased him with funny faces. She took the little toy car and followed a make-believe road across his legs and arms, imitating the sounds of a rattling engine and screeching brakes. I stood over Mary's shoulder and watched the little boy's eyes follow her hands. Mary kept on until a feeble smile slipped across the mouth of his sad little face. Mary had broken through. Within minutes that boy had all the presents sprawled across his lap. And for the first time, the hospital staff saw and heard him giggling with delight. People began gathering around to see what was so amusing. Here was Mary with that little guy—both of them talking a mile a minute—him in Croatian (the language of Bosnia) and Mary in hillbilly English. Neither one of them had a clue what the other was saying, but there they were, Mary's eyes reflecting the twinkle in his, as they bantered back and forth, communicating through the universal language—love.

As I watched Mary perform wonders with these kids, I began to note her technique. She always made eye contact with each child, but even more important was her personal touch—whether a warm hug, a reassuring squeeze, or a tender pat on a little face staring up into hers. She made a point to treat each one exactly the same—special! Mary was not offended by their dirt, nor was she sickened by their dreadful smell. Her affection, in many cases, was the only medicine these little ones needed. Her compassion proved that "A *merry heart does good, like medicine*" (Prov. 17:22).

"Mary, how is it that you have so much love for these kids?" I asked her later that day.

She said, "Brother Franklin, I see myself in these people. Like them, I growed up hard, had a tough childhood. We didn't have money. We stayed hungry. In the wintertime we couldn't keep warm. I know what they're a goin' through."

I began to see some similarities between the hollers of West Virginia and the mountains of Bosnia. I guess Mary felt at home. And the Bosnian people sensed their common bond.

Folks often make excuses about why God can't use them: "I can't speak their language—they won't understand me." "Their skin is a different color than mine—they won't accept me." "How can I relate to their problems?"

Mary couldn't speak the language of the Bosnian people but she found a way to "love on them a little bit." That, they understood. She was there reaching out with love and compassion. As the

British would say, she was willing to "give it a go" in spite of the obstacles—like being a poor country girl.

Mary may have been reluctant to go to the White House, but once she got there, she wasn't intimidated in the company of the President about asking him if she could pray—she knew that God would hear her prayer. She wasn't terrified to reach out and speak to a child who couldn't understand—she knew that God would translate her love to that little one. Mary had learned an important lesson: Use the gifts God has given and be willing to give it a go. God will do the rest. She was simply a tool in the hand of the One who communicates to each heart that is opened up to Him.

What about you? Are you willing to give it a go? If so, you can begin to make an impact on others. Mary didn't allow her state of affairs to hold her back. She didn't blame her environment for not having the opportunities in life others were given. Instead she learned like the apostle Paul: *"I know what it is to be in need. . . . I have learned the secret of being content in any and every situation"* (Phil. 4:12 NIV).

GOD HAS A CALLING FOR YOU

Hillbillies are a slice of Americana—and some of the country's most upstanding citizens. I'm personally proud of my hillbilly roots; I was born and raised in the mountains of western North Carolina. We have our own customs, our own way of saying things, and our own sense of humor. But our society isn't particularly accepting of countrified folks.

What is it about Mary? She's lived a hard life. It's not her wealth; her husband is a laid-off coal miner who has the beginnings of black lung disease. It isn't her position in society. Deeper than those mountain ravines from which she hails is God's love, which has empowered Mary to conquer her feeling of inadequacy. It has given her an incredible sense of mission and the ability to live a life beyond the limits of the poverty of the Appalachian coal country.

Regardless of your social standing, God has a calling for you—whether poor and uneducated or living in luxury and ease, God can use you if you'll give it a go.

Mary was available to the Lord. Availability has been defined as "being willing to start where you are, use what you have, and do the best you can." If that's the attitude you have, then God can do immeasurably more than all we ask or imagine, according to His power that is at work within us (Eph. 3:20).

If Mary had waited until her family's financial needs were completely met, she would have never filled a single shoe box. If she had waited until she could obtain a proper wardrobe or get a college degree, she would have missed what God had in store for this moment in time.

Don't limit yourself in God's service simply because you come from a small town, the inner city, or a place tucked away in hopelessness. It is just like God to take the smallest and least of His creation and turn it into something great and significant. It makes no difference where you are from. All that really counts is, Where are you going? Why are you going? and Who is going with you? After all, God never makes a mistake.

If you're in sync with God, He will empower you and arm you with all that's necessary to give it a go.

Each one should use whatever gift he has received to serve others, faithfully administering God's grace in its various forms. If anyone speaks, he should do it as one speaking the very words of God. If anyone serves, he should do it with the strength God provides, so that in all things God may be praised through Jesus Christ. (1 Peter 4:10–11 NIV)

He never starts something that He doesn't finish.

B E I R U T   I N   B L O O D

O NE, TWO, THREE, JUMP!" *This is crazy,* I thought, as I
hurled my body from the leaky freighter into the small
dinghy tied up alongside.

I was trying to sneak into Lebanon, no small feat in the early
eighties during the height of their civil war. Sami Dagher had
called, asking me to come.

"There's no way in, Sami," I had protested. But with Sami there
is always a way.

The airport in Beirut was closed, and all land routes were off
limits, strategically monitored by the military. Sami convinced me
to fly to Cyprus. "Then, my brother, you can take a boat from
there" Sami assured me, "to *just off the coast of Lebanon.*" I had
been wanting to visit Sami, so his rationale convinced me to pack
my bags and head for the Middle East.

It was a cold, rainy January afternoon when the plane touched
down in Cyprus. I had landed at the airport in Larnaca and headed
straight for the dock where I boarded an old cargo ship well after
dark. I had no idea what the next few hours held in store. The rust
bucket set sail around midnight, timed to arrive by 10:00 the next
morning.

"Just off the coast of Lebanon" turned out to be about five miles
away from the dock, just out of range of the Syrian artillery posted

up on the mountain peaks that jutted out high above the coastline city of Beirut. The Syrians didn't think twice about opening fire on any ship that came in too close.

The old boat made its way across the Mediterranean Sea. As Lebanon's shore came into hazy view, I scanned the blustery waters of the sea, knowing that the time had come to transfer from the cargo ship to a smaller boat that would eventually take us to dry land. These little skiffs were commanded by men as rough as the waves. Their fearlessness gave passengers a calm sense of assurance that we would get safely inland—that is, if we were able to make a precision leap from one vessel to another.

The giant swells kept slamming each little dinghy up against the rusted hull of the freighter, forcing the boats to ride the waves before coming back in close to the ship. If the jump wasn't timed just right, you'd miss the tiny boat on its way back out to sea and find yourself fighting the black and untamed cold waters of a January Mediterranean. Worse, if you timed your jump too soon, you might get caught in between the dinghy and the freighter as one crashed into the other, squashing you like a bug.

Studying the tumultuous sea, I took a deep breath and hurled myself over the edge of the ship and across the foaming waters. With a satisfying thud I felt my feet hit the deck. *The worst part of the trip is behind me,* I thought, as I watched our dinghy drift quickly away from the ship. That feeling didn't stay with me too long, because the nearer we inched toward the coastline, the more I questioned the wisdom of revisiting this war-torn country. As I looked back over my shoulder, I realized that just as I had committed myself to the little dinghy, now I must commit my heart to the task that was ahead.

I hunkered down in the boat and looked around into the faces of my traveling companions. Many were well dressed, but their rumpled clothing and the two-day stubble on their faces added to their weary appearance. What could possibly be important enough to bring them to Lebanon at this particular time? Maybe they wondered the same about me.

As our boat navigated closer to the little harbor, I prayed, "Well, Lord, here I am. Please show me what You want me to do (*besides worry about the Syrian guns stationed inland*)."

If we were fortunate enough to escape gunfire, the greeting "Welcome to Beirut" did not necessarily mean that we were home free. This once beautiful city had fallen into tatters. In 1980 Beirut was the most dangerous city on earth. Car bombs and drive-by shootings along Sniper Alley were common, not to mention artillery barrages that would level sections of the city. And kidnapping Americans was fair game.

Lebanon no longer had a functioning government, so immigration formalities didn't exist—passports were not an issue. If you could dodge the bullets and find someone crazy enough to bring you ashore, you could get in. As a matter of fact, they'd pat you on the back and say, "Welcome," with a big grin. But what they really meant was, "You foolish sucker."

In spite of the danger and chaos, the Lebanese mountains were more magnificent than postcard snapshots. Once again, it felt good to be back in Lebanon—a country I have come to love.

Many have asked why I'm so fond of this little spot on earth. It can pretty much be wrapped up in the person of Sami Dagher. Every time I set foot on Lebanon's soil, I find myself reminiscing about this powerful man of remarkable faith.

Sami Dagher is a Lebanese Christian believer and a close friend of mine. I recall after completing a project in Baghdad following the Gulf War, Sami told me he was hoping to return to Baghdad to preach the gospel. Some friends of his protested that it was much too dangerous. "Besides, Sami," they reminded him, "you're sixty years old. Why don't you just take it easy? You deserve some rest."

Sami replied that being older was the very *reason* he should go, not an excuse to avoid going. "Better that I should die than a young missionary who has many years left to preach the gospel," he said.

So many things went through my mind as the boat safely docked. All that mattered to me at that moment was the sight of Sami awaiting my arrival. Seeing his smile made the long, dreary trip worthwhile.

Driving through the streets of the capital with Sami is always an experience. He didn't waste any time filling me in on the latest bombings and assassinations. But what was really on his heart was the recent casualties unleashed against two refugee camps just outside the city limits, Sabra and Shatila. As I listened to Sami describe the atrocities, I knew that this was my ultimate call while in Lebanon—to see for myself what God might have us do. He had something very special in mind, not only for Sami and his Lebanese brothers, but also for the Palestinians.

With the sea breeze at our backs, we headed straight for Sami's church for a brief rest before continuing on.

The Massacre that Shocked the World

Ariel Sharon walks like a bulldozer rolls. The eyes of the world had been on him and his country, Israel, as their army crashed into southern Lebanon, aligning themselves with the Lebanese Christian Militia (known as the Phalangists). It was 1982, and the Palestine Liberation Organization (the PLO), which had the support of Russia and the entire Arab world, had taken control of southern Lebanon. They were being backed into these two small refugee camps outside of Beirut by General Sharon's forces.

For seven years, the Christian population in Lebanon had paid with their blood, their wives, and their children for living under the PLO rule. The Phalangists' leader, President-elect Bashir Gemayel, had been assassinated a few days earlier, so the passions between the two opposing forces were running white-hot.

Now the Palestinians were cornered. This was the Phalangists' chance to get even. Each member of the Lebanese militia fought as one. Each was intimately acquainted with a relative or friend who had fallen under the brutality of the PLO. Instead of taking control of the escalating situation, General Sharon (for reasons not clear) allowed the Lebanese militia to have complete reign over Sabra and Shatila. Ostensibly, their mission was to mop up the Palestinian guerrillas who had fled there to hide.

The massacre that had followed shocked the world. The Israelis turned their backs as seven hundred to eight hundred Palestinian men, women, and children were heartlessly killed. Though the massacre temporarily broke the back of the PLO, leaving them scared, frightened, and demoralized, it was one of the last official decisions that General Sharon made as Israel's defense minister. The episode created a shrilling public outcry that he could not overcome. He resigned in disgrace.

When the facts of the massacre became known, the world's anger was matched only by its surprise. This was not like Israel. Perhaps because of Israel's history of being oppressed, mistreated, and abused, the world had come to know Israel as a nation of people who fought hard but fairly, an army that was a fierce foe but a compassionate victor. Except in the case of one particularly notorious Nazi war criminal, Adolf Eichmann, the Israeli government wouldn't even consider capital punishment.

But the haunting eyes of the surviving Palestinian children, the muffled sobs of the women, and the debilitating despair of the men were vivid testimonies that all sense of human compassion had withered before venomous hatred as the Phalangists unleashed their fury. What happened in these two refugee camps was not about control of land; it was about revenge.

As we sat in the church office discussing the devastation, I said, "Sami, we've got to go into Sabra and Shatila."

"Oh, my brother," Sami replied, in horror, "it is too dangerous."

"Sami, we need to preach Christ to them. These people have been defeated; they're afraid; they have lost everything. What an opportunity for us to reach them. Besides, what in Lebanon isn't dangerous?"

He laughed cautiously, knowing there was no sense in arguing the point.

Keep in mind that I was asking a *Lebanese Christian* to go into the camps. In the eyes of the Palestinians, Sami Dagher was the enemy. Many of the surviving refugees would probably have preferred to put a bullet through the forehead of a Lebanese Christian rather than to shake his hand. But Sami is courageous, willing to be open for any opportunity to preach the gospel. I knew Sami would not let me go in alone.

The refugee camps were on the outskirts of the city. As we drove through the streets, I felt I had landed on a distant planet. The camps wept misery; they were a pathetic ruin. Large sections of the cheap, cinder-block walls had been run over. The barbed wire that was supposed to keep enemies out was now twisted up and sprawling over broken walls, a vivid testimony to its inability to withstand unwanted invaders.

Once inside the demolished camp of Shatila, the sights grew even worse. Rusted rebar stuck out from the roofs and walls of bombed-out buildings. Some houses were literally cut in two, exposing the rooms to the outside world. After the Phalangists had tired of pulling triggers, they decided to assault the camps with bulldozers; they had ripped up buildings, dug up foundations, and twisted roof supports into grotesque shapes. There wasn't a single house that hadn't fallen prey to the soldiers' malice.

And the smell. Burst sewer pipes spewed raw sewage down the streets, which eventually collected in offensive pools. And though the sight of the destruction was contemptible and the smell of the demolition was oppressive, the people were too afraid to leave even this wretched camp. If the soldiers would do this to them inside their makeshift village, they thought, what fate might await them outside?

By virtually any government official's account, both Sabra and Shatila would have been considered a slum and a squalor even before they were attacked; but whatever semblance of dignity the refugees had sought to build for themselves was now utterly lost.

ONE HAND CAN'T CLAP

We were stunned that no one prevented our vehicle from going right into Shatila. There were no sentries, no guard posts. A couple of months earlier, we would have been shot for doing this, or at least hauled into a Palestinian prison for interrogation.

We drove a couple hundred yards through rubble and stopped the car outside a house that had been cut in two. The severed shell reminded me of the back of a little girl's playhouse. The main difference, of course, was that this was someone's place of refuge.

A Palestinian man peered over the edge of the second floor and saw us. He was curious as to why we had come. He didn't let the collapsed stairwell keep him from coming down to meet us; he quickly climbed down the homemade wooden ladder.

What do you say to a man whose world has been bombed? Hallmark doesn't make greeting cards for situations such as this, believe me. I stood by my car and nodded as the man approached us. His English was broken, but certainly better than my Arabic.

"What happened to your house?" I asked.

"Bulldozers," the man said, his lower lip quivering.

I told him how sorry we were and asked if he could make the repairs needed.

The man looked down shaking his head. He then lifted his feeble hand and pointed to the rest of the camp. Tears pushed their way up from the bottom of both his eyes. "Look at this," he said, his bony hand sweeping the camp. "Just look at this."

It was as if he was walking around in a daze but somehow managing to hang on to his sanity.

I turned to Sami and said, "These people may have been your enemy, Sami, but what an opportunity to tell them about God's love—about His Son, Jesus Christ. We can't turn our backs on these people."

"My brother," Sami said, "one hand can't clap by itself. You need two hands. I cannot come here and work by myself."

"Sami, if you can find the people to help, I will go back home and try to raise the money needed."

Sami's face reflected the absolute resolve that I had come to love. I slapped him on the back as he said, "My brother, if you will provide the funds, I will do whatever it takes to help these people."

There was a young inexperienced missionary who had been sent to Lebanon by his mission. He had asked Sami if he could come along to see the camps. Sami had agreed, thinking that the exposure to life in the refugee camps would be an eye-opener for him. Now, I have seen some heroically committed missionaries in my time, men and women who have left everything to go to a foreign country and in some cases sacrificed their lives to reach the hurting and the unsaved. But this young man seemed to be out of touch. He had a camera slung around his neck and was taking pictures of the devastation that surrounded us. He was down on his knees, focusing his lens and his attention on the debris, hoping to frame the photographs effectively, instead of focusing his heart on the old man's broken life.

I watched him out of the corner of my eye as long as I could, then turned and asked him how he planned to help Sami reach out in this camp.

He was too busy clicking his camera to hear.

I called out to him louder, "What are you going to do?"

He finally lowered his camera, looked at me, and said with satisfaction, "I'm going to write a report and send it with my pictures back to headquarters."

My heart sank. What an opportunity this young man was missing. Samaritan's Purse had offered the funds, Sami had made the commitment to return, but where would we get the people to distribute the medicine and food that were desperately needed? And even more important, where would we find men to proclaim the gospel? Even with these questions left unanswered, Sami and I were determined to move forward.

If we truly want to go beyond the limits, we must be willing to act decisively when opportunities come, even when that means reaching out to our enemy.

BONDS FORGED BY LOVE

Over the next several months, Sami was eventually able to gather a small group of men from his church and deliver thousands of food parcels to the refugees. Through the help of Samaritan's Purse, Sami brought doctors into the camp to treat the sick; volunteers repaired or replaced roofs and windows. For six months, the Palestinian Muslims were shocked that Lebanese believers were feeding them. When Sami knocked on the door of one man's home, he was met with a skeptical, even violent look. When he held out the food parcel, however, the Palestinian man's face broke into a wide smile and Sami was quickly and enthusiastically invited in.

The man's son, a little three-year-old boy named Mohammed, was very sick. Children are always hit the hardest in such camps—their frail immune systems are poor rivals for vicious, oftentimes fatal diseases. Mohammed looked like he would soon join the children who die before they ever really know what it's like to live. Sami grew particularly alarmed when he noticed that the child's eyes were sinking deep into the sockets. The young boy looked like a corpse.

"I will bring a doctor back today," Sami told the mother. She started crying. "Thank you, oh thank you very much."

And there, in that dirty, bombed-out, and disease-ridden camp, a Palestinian Muslim shook the hand of a Lebanese believer.

Reconciliation had come. If it could happen in that one home, it could happen many times over as lives are touched by the power of the gospel put into action.

In the months ahead, a handful of Palestinians professed Jesus Christ as their Savior. The practical care and compassion of the Lebanese believers resulted in the formation of a little evangelical church in the midst of a Palestinian enclave. Love was actively breaching the walls of prejudice that had existed for thousands of years. However, the camp's leaders, who had done very little to address the refugees' needs, discovered what was going on.

These extremists began to see Sami's work as a serious threat to their own power and influence. How could they portray the Lebanese Christians as the enemy when they were the only ones bringing food, medicine, and assistance? It wasn't long before Sami began receiving death threats and was warned not to return to the camps. Tensions were rising again in Beirut. The PLO had been defeated; however, new and more extreme groups were beginning to emerge. One such group was known as Hizballah (meaning "party of God"), with strong ties to Iran. The Hizballah became a violent and potent force in the suburbs of Beirut.

Not long after the U.S. Embassy and Marine headquarters were bombed, the gates to the Sabra and Shatila camps were slammed shut. Allied forces pulled back, and the PLO rose Phoenix-like out of the ashes.

Yet bonds forged by love are always stronger than the chasms created by hate. Whenever the shelling would start between east Beirut (predominantly Christian) and west Beirut (predominantly Muslim), people would run for shelter. When the shelling subsided for an hour or so, the Lebanese phone lines testified to an almost comical unity. Sami would get a call from a Palestinian believer in the camps: "Brother Sami, we're so sorry that our wicked cousins are shelling your city. How are you? Nobody is hurt, are they? We're praying for you."

"And we're praying for you," Sami would say with a catch in his voice, and before hanging up, they would pray together. Because Sami chose to obey God, he exceeded the limits of animosity and fulfilled 1 Peter 3:8–9: "*Live in harmony with one another; be sympathetic, love as brothers, be compassionate and humble. Do not repay evil with evil or insult with insult, but with blessing, because to this you were called*" (NIV).

A MAN OF ACTION

By the time that young missionary's report reached the desk of an administrator, the opportunity to reach out to Sabra and Shatila had long since passed. It has been said that opportunities multiply as they are seized; they die when neglected.

Sometimes God opens doors, but they do not stay open forever. We may not recognize these little windows of opportunity if we are out of sync with God. We need to stay very close to Him, moment by moment.

Because Sami's life was in sync with God, his heart was receptive to God's prompting, and Sami responded in obedience. When I see Sami in action, I always recall the story of the Good Samaritan.

> *A certain man went down from Jerusalem to Jericho, and fell among thieves, who stripped him of his clothing, wounded him, and departed, leaving him half dead. Now by chance a certain priest came down that road. And when he saw him, he passed by on the other side. Likewise a Levite, when he arrived at the place, came and looked, and passed*

by on the other side. But a certain Samaritan, as he journeyed, came where he was. And when he saw him, he had compassion. (Luke 10:30–33)

You have to understand, in the Bible a Samaritan was a second-class citizen despised by the Jews. It took a supernatural love for a despised Samaritan to look past centuries of ridicule, persecution, and discrimination to reach out to a Jew.

The Levite didn't reach out to the man in need. Perhaps he intended to send a representative back to the man whom he saw lying by the side of the road. Maybe he was trying to make a quick assessment—the first-century equivalent of taking photographs.

And maybe the priest was moved in his heart to make plans to form a Stricken Travelers' Ministry, where his synagogue members would patrol the highways and offer assistance. He was too busy to help this particular man, of course, but maybe, someday, he could really do something about this bothersome highway-robbery thing . . .

Who knows?

But Jesus said that it was only the Good Samaritan who discovered the secret of love—the one who did something for the beaten man, reaching out beyond the barriers of prejudice and ministering to a hurting man's practical needs. That's the man who follows in the footsteps of our Lord.

The man God uses is a man of action. He doesn't make excuses or wait for better weather or a more appropriate time. He is a man who sees what needs to be done and then does it—in spite of the fact that he might be helping his worst enemy.

It took a supernatural love for Sami to overcome his mistrust of the Palestinians. The people Sami reached out to had instigated a civil war that left Beirut—Sami's hometown—barely tolerable by any standards. It would have been much more comfortable for Sami to witness the devastation of the Sabra and Shatila camps and say, *They finally got what they deserved, Lord. Thank You for Your judgment.*

The fact is, the Bible says that all have sinned, *"There is no one righteous, not even one"* (Rom. 3:10 NIV). Sami realized that his own people, the Lebanese, were as deserving of God's judgment as were the Palestinians, so he followed Christ's teaching and offered a cup of cool water to his enemy in the name of the Lord. *"And if anyone gives even a cup of cold water to one of these little ones because he is my disciple, I tell you the truth, he will certainly not lose his reward"* (Matt. 10:42 NIV).

This is exactly why Jesus' teaching was so offensive to the Pharisees. For centuries, they lived by "an eye for an eye, and a tooth for a tooth." But Jesus turned that completely around, from a negative to a positive: *"Love your neighbor as yourself"* (Mark 12:31 NIV).

Sami often challenges people by asking, "What is the purpose of life? Why are we here? Just to breathe so many cubic centimeters of oxygen and eat so many kilos of beef?" If we are going to advance the cause of Jesus Christ in areas of the world where the gospel has not penetrated, it will take men and women willing to put themselves aside and walk with God regardless of where those footsteps may lead.

That may mean reaching beyond our church walls; beyond our race, perhaps; certainly, beyond our close circle of friends. We'll have to learn how to take the love of God to those who count themselves our enemies, to those who might even wish us harm.

And if you really want to touch the heart of God and live life beyond the limits—look for your enemy, and treat him like your friend. The outcome may surprise you. *"When a man's ways please the LORD, he makes even his enemies to be at peace with him"* (Prov. 16:7).

A WANTED MAN

In October 1995 my father and I received a joint invitation to hold an area-wide crusade in Saskatoon, Saskatchewan, Canada. We both accepted, but as time grew closer, Daddy wasn't sure he'd be able to make it. He was holding a crusade the week prior in Sacramento, California, and after such a strenuous week he wasn't sure his health and strength would allow him to preach another crusade so soon.

"Daddy," I said, "we'll leave it up to the Lord. If you can come— come."

This was the first time we would have an opportunity to preach together. If it happened, it would be a highlight for me, but to be honest, I was nervous at the prospect.

When my father finished in Sacramento, I received a call from him. "I'm on my way to Saskatoon." I was thrilled to know he felt strong enough to come. We agreed that I would preach the first three nights and that he would preach the last service, which happened to be on Sunday. On Saturday afternoon, just a few hours before the evening meeting, my father, who had already arrived in the city, called me in my hotel room and asked, "Can you come up and see me?"

When I got to his room, he said, "Franklin, I have received a number of letters from different members of my board of directors.

They're all saying I need to make a decision about what will happen to this ministry should I retire or should something happen to my health that would prevent me from continuing.

"I've given this much thought and prayer and feel you're the one who should lead this organization into the future. When the board meets in two weeks, I would like to recommend that you succeed me as chairman and chief executive officer of the Billy Graham Evangelistic Association [BGEA]. If they approve this recommendation, would you be willing to accept this responsibility?"

I looked into my father's intense eyes. His ministry has been a part of my life since I was born. I have served on his board of directors since 1979, and most of that time I have also served on his executive committee. I know the inner workings of the BGEA as well as anybody. I love my father and the gospel that he has been so faithful to preach.

As a son I feel it's my duty to be willing to do whatever it takes to help my father. More important, I know that I must follow God's leading in my life. The Lord has called me to preach. I know that with this invitation comes a huge load of responsibility, and one that I cannot fulfill without God's daily guidance.

I can never replace my father. No one can. He is a unique and gifted man. I want to encourage him to preach as long as he has the health and strength to do so. This was not an invitation to be the next Billy Graham. This was a request to take the leadership of an organization committed to the proclamation of the gospel. It means a lot to know that my father would trust me to lead the BGEA.

"Yes," I answered slowly, "I will accept that position if the board asks." A smile came across my father's face as if a burden had been lifted. The future of the organization weighs heavily on his shoulders. "Daddy, I pledge to you that I will not take the BGEA to the left or to the right. I will keep the Billy Graham Evangelistic Association's focus centered in evangelism, preaching, and proclaiming the gospel of the Lord Jesus Christ, all of my life."

After much discussion and a time of prayer at the board meeting on November 7, 1995, the directors voted unanimously for me to take the leadership of the BGEA as chairman of the board and CEO of the corporation when my father decides to step aside. I realized that the confidence the board placed in me was a great honor.

All of us have a human need to be wanted, to be loved, to be accepted, and to measure up—especially in a father's eyes. Fourteen months later, though, I would experience an entirely different sense of being a wanted man.

On February 5, 1997, I was on my way to Minnesota for meetings at my father's office. Daddy has asked me to visit his Minneapolis office staff as often as possible so I would become better acquainted with the managers and their families. I was on Highway 19 East, headed to the airport in Carter County, Tennessee. Suddenly I noticed some swirling blue lights in my rearview mirror.

What's this all about? I wondered, and pulled over to let the sheriff's deputy pass. When his patrol car followed me onto the shoulder, I was surprised to discover that he was after me!

The deputy approached the car as I rolled the window down. His mustache disguised his young face. "What's the matter, officer?" I asked.

"You were following the car ahead of you too closely. I need to see your driver's license and registration." He nervously held out his hand.

"You've got to be kidding! You were way behind me! How could you see if I was too close or not?"

The deputy was now visibly shaken and hesitantly said, "Your driver's license and registration please."

"You must be having a real slow day," I said with a smile.

"I've been told to write tickets," he answered apologetically. "Your driver's license and registration please."

"Well, guess you have to do what you're told." I laughed and pulled out my wallet.

The officer was quiet as he started writing. When he finished, he ripped off the top sheet of his pad and handed it to me. I looked at the citation for the set fine, but all that was noted was a summons to appear in court on the twenty-fourth of the month. I knew there was no use to argue, so I crammed the paper down in my pocket and hit the pavement, carefully watching the road behind me.

My mind whirled. The twenty-fourth? For some time I had been scheduled to be in Alaska, so when I returned to my office a few days later, I called a local attorney in Carter County and explained my dilemma.

"No problem, Franklin," he assured me. "I'll call the district attorney and get his advice."

When he called back, he assured me, "The district attorney said everything is okay. Go on to Alaska. I'll be in court to represent you, and we'll ask for a continuance."

I went to Alaska, assuming this little traffic incident was behind me. I couldn't have been more wrong.

Wanted: Franklin Graham

A few weeks later, I had just returned home from Alaska when a friend faxed the front page of the Elizabethton, Tennessee, newspaper to me, which carried a bold headline: BILLY GRAHAM'S SON WANTED BY CARTER COUNTY COURT.

This has got to be a joke, I thought. Within a few moments, the phone rang and the attorney was on the line. "Franklin," he said, "we have a problem."

"You got that right! What in the world went wrong? Weren't you in court representing me?"

"Franklin, this is very strange. I can't ever remember this happening. They don't give out arrest warrants for tailgating, but in your case it looks like that's exactly what they've done."

"This is crazy."

The attorney sighed. "Franklin, in my opinion the judge is trying to use this for his own political means. With you being a public person, he decided to issue an arrest warrant when you failed to appear in traffic court, even though I was there to represent you."

"Well, we have a problem and we better get it fixed, sooner than later," I said.

As I hung up the phone, I had second thoughts about this particular attorney's ability to represent me. I could imagine going to Carter County, being arrested, and being placed in handcuffs, my picture displayed in all kinds of newspapers. That was not the kind of publicity I was looking for! And I can tell you, that's not something my father would be too thrilled to see in print. On the other hand, Mama would probably laugh and think it was all a lot of fun.

I called another attorney friend of mine, Randall Groves down in Charlotte, and explained the situation to him. He agreed that I needed to see the judge as soon as possible.

"Franklin," he warned me, "whatever you do, don't tick him off. Keep your answers short. Say yes, sir, and no, sir. He can make your life real unpleasant, understand?"

"I get the picture."

I couldn't believe this was happening. If they had just given me a ticket I could send back in the mail, I would have gladly paid the fine, but I didn't even know what the fine was. All I got was a citation and a court date.

I better go down there today, I thought. Elizabethton is only about an hour from my office, but I had a friend drive me in a different car. I was not going to risk another ticket.

We arrived shortly before 5:00. A local pilot friend of mine, Bob Glover, who helped teach me how to fly the MU2 and is one of the more experienced MU2 pilots in the country, met me at the courthouse and was mad as a hornet about what had happened.

Bob had his boss, Bill Green, one of Carter County's leading citizens, and owner of the local Carter County bank, join me for support in the courtroom. Bill sits on the board of directors of several universities and is very much involved politically on the state and county level.

The courtroom was empty when we went in; the attorney and sheriff's deputy walked in behind us.

"All rise," the sheriff's deputy intoned.

We stood.

The judge entered from his chambers.

"You may be seated," the bailiff said.

I remembered Randall Grove's strong counsel, "Don't tick the judge off."

The attorney stood and spoke to the judge, who motioned for him to come to the bench. The attorney advised me to follow.

"Do you understand the charges against you, Mr. Graham?" the judge asked.

"Yes," I said.

"You have the right to remain silent . . ."

I couldn't believe I was actually hearing somebody read me my rights! Finally, the judge said, "I'll rescind the capias"—which would remove the arrest warrant—"and set a date for you to appear before my court."

"Yes sir," I said, pulling out my calendar as he studied his appointment book. We settled on a date in May that would work for all concerned.

We left the court and went directly to the attorney's office to discuss the matter. Bill Green pulled the attorney aside and scolded him. "Listen," he said, "you have dropped the ball on this one. Our county's gonna look like the *Dukes of Hazard*, putting Franklin in the paper and making him come back for a trial over tailgating. This is ridiculous." Then he asked, "How much is the fine if he opts to pay it?"

The attorney reached behind his desk where he had a large volume of law books. He pulled one down and flipped through the thick book and said, "The fine is two dollars."

"You mean to tell me that Franklin has to take a whole day to appear in court about a dispute over a two-dollar fine?! Let me tell you what you're going to do. You're going back to that judge and find out what it will take to resolve this. Otherwise, you are going to have the tabloids, not to mention everyone else, writing about this. It will make us look like a bunch of country bumpkins, including the judge. We sure don't need that."

Bright and early the next morning, the attorney was at the judge's office. He explained to him that this matter would turn into a media circus if it wasn't handled quickly. It wouldn't look good for him, and it certainly wouldn't look good for the county. Was there any way this could be resolved without another court appearance?

The judge suggested that I post a bond of $104.50 for the court costs, and $2.00 for the fine. Then I could forfeit the bond and that would resolve the matter—saving the county, and me, a lot of embarrassment. Though many citizens called the courthouse offering to take care of the fine on my behalf, I was glad to pay it just to have the matter resolved once and for all.

LESSONS

Believe it or not, I learned from this incident. *First,* I couldn't believe the exposure that this arrest warrant received for a measly two-dollar infraction. This story was picked up by cable TV, the Associated Press, and local television and radio. It boggles my mind that these media outlets can send out relatively trivial news like this within minutes. Never before in the history of the world has information been disseminated so quickly and easily.

When George Washington fought the Revolutionary War, he sometimes had to wait days to receive information concerning momentous political and military victories and defeats. Today, he'd know the body count before the smoke of the battlefield had cleared. During the Civil War, news of a loved one's death could take weeks to make its way back and finally be listed in the local papers. Today, telegrams notifying families that someone is missing or killed in action can arrive within hours. When Princess Diana died in an automobile accident in Paris, news of the tragedy was flashed across the airwaves within minutes.

But if you think this is daunting, consider the final judgment. The Bible tells us that *"whatever you have spoken in the dark will be heard in the light, and what you have spoken in the ear in inner rooms will be proclaimed on the housetops"* (Luke 12:3). I was amazed that news of a small fine levied in Carter County, Tennessee, could make its way across the country—but the Bible forewarns us that revelations of the softest whisper will make their way up to heaven, where they'll be proclaimed for all to hear.

In other words, the appearance of holiness just won't cut it. It never has. Someone will blow the whistle eventually. Congressman J. C. Watts has been quoted as saying, "Character is doing right when no one is looking." There are no secrets with God. He not only picks up the quietest whisper, but He *"judges the thoughts and attitudes of the heart. Nothing in all creation is hidden from God's sight. Everything is uncovered and laid bare before the eyes of him to whom we must give account"* (Heb. 4:12–13 NIV).

My ticket and the resulting arrest warrant and media exposure were a good reminder that none of us can be too careful because people will stoop to set traps in our pathways. Satan also has his traps. He wants to embarrass you—to discredit your life and testimony and bring you down, along with the name of Jesus Christ— if he can. But the Bible admonishes us in 2 Corinthians 8:21 to take *"pains to do what is right, not only in the eyes of the Lord but also in the eyes of men"* (NIV).

Second, the most seemingly innocent violations can cause unforeseen consequences. I found out that the tiniest transgression can be blown out of proportion and soon get out of control. My two-dollar fine—which couldn't even buy a meal at McDonald's—resulted in the request of two separate court appearances, an arrest warrant, and ultimately a payment of $106.50.

How can we go beyond the limits of allowing the apparently little things to get the best of us? The book of Isaiah tells us to heed the voice of the Lord, *"Your ears will hear a voice behind you, saying, 'This is the way; walk in it'"* (30:21 NIV). We can have confidence that God is leading us minute by minute if we turn our ear toward Him. He will always be there to show us the way.

> *Enter by the narrow gate; for wide is the gate and broad is the way that leads to destruction, and there are many who go in by it. Because narrow is the gate and difficult is the way which leads to life, and there are few who find it.* (Matt. 7:13–14)

Where is this narrow road? I once heard a preacher say that the narrow road went right down the middle of a big open highway with passengers cruising the opposite direction.

Sins are often perceived as incidental mistakes, but when they are found out, Easy Street isn't all that it's cracked up to be. Many times it's filled with potholes and diversions.

"The highway of the upright avoids evil; he who guards his way guards his life" (Prov. 16:17 NIV). We are ultimately responsible for our actions, so we better take full account of each mile we travel.

Third, we tend to dismiss the tiny slipups, but we have to remember that God's standard is perfection, and His judgment is all that counts. The judge makes the ultimate decision, and in my case, he had the legal right to issue a warrant for my arrest. By his interpretation I had violated the law. Now, people don't usually end up in prison for tailgating or failing to pay a two-dollar fine. I thought I had my obligation covered by clearing my absence with the local attorney; I soon found out that the judge has the authority to issue the final ruling.

That's how it will be in heaven. You may have been told by a well-meaning Christian, "Oh, don't feel guilty about that. That's not *really* a sin," but you may be surprised at the final judgment. Maybe you've even heard a pastor rationalize your behavior. But one evil thought, one lie, or one slip of the tongue is all it takes to keep us out of heaven for eternity if we do not repent and turn from our wicked ways. No one is exempt.

I remember back in 1974, my father was holding a congress on evangelism in Lausanne, Switzerland. One evening as he was preaching in the Lausanne Stadium he told about receiving three parking tickets while in Switzerland. Apparently each time he parked, the meter ran out by just a few minutes. He had to pay a fine for each ticket because he violated the law. He didn't mean to let the meter run out, but that did not excuse the fact that his time had expired. I'll never forget him saying, "We don't get away with breaking the law in Switzerland—neither do we get away with breaking God's law."

As Christians we are called to a higher standard. What is that standard? To live in such a way that no one can find fault with our lives as we walk with Christ. "*Whatever happens, conduct yourselves in a manner worthy of the gospel of Christ*" (Phil. 1:27 NIV), "*so that our ministry will not be discredited*" (2 Cor. 6:3 NIV).

GOD CAN USE A CHICKEN

W HERE DID THAT GUY GO? I was traveling through the airport in Munich, Germany, with Ricky Skaggs, the renowned bluegrass/country music artist. We were returning from a trip on behalf of Operation Christmas Child. We were both exhausted. We had left Sarajevo the day before at 4:00 A.M. and had driven through the rugged Bosnian mountains down to the Dalmatian coast of Croatia to the city of Split, where we caught a Croatian Airlines flight to Zagreb for the night. We had slept a few hours, and then the next morning caught a 6:00 A.M. flight to Munich.

It was a cold December day, and we were glad to be inside the airport terminal. Both of us were hoping to take advantage of the forty-five-minute layover to do some last minute Christmas shopping at the airport.

As we hurried through the crowded corridors, we spotted a young woman sitting in a corner, crying. *She probably just said good-bye to her husband,* I thought, and kept walking. You see tears at airports all the time. If you stopped every time you saw someone crying, you'd never leave.

I turned to say something to Ricky, but he was gone. I stopped in my tracks, wondering, *Where in the world is he?* When I looked around, Ricky was kneeling beside the despondent lady.

My shoulders dropped, and, with a slight tolerant breath, I walked over to see what was going on.

"Can I help you?" Ricky gently asked her.

I was impatient. *Come on, Ricky,* I said to myself. *We'll never get out of here if you talk to everyone who is crying!*

Ricky patiently questioned the woman, who fortunately spoke English. He learned that she was in transit from another country and had lost her airline ticket. She felt stranded and didn't know what to do.

"Let me see if I can help you," Ricky said. "Come with me."

I'm shy when it comes to approaching a total stranger, but it didn't bother Ricky at all. He took control of the situation and led the woman to an airline official and asked for help. He didn't leave her side until he had complete assurance she would be cared for. As he excused himself, he wished her a merry Christmas, then headed back my way with a grin all over his face.

He walked up alongside, slapped me on the back, and said, "You know, Franklin, 'Christmas time's a comin'" (the title of a bluegrass song he sings).

I shook my head, knowing in my heart that the little interruption really hadn't inconvenienced us at all. We still had plenty of time to do our shopping and board the plane on time. Later, as we rumbled down the runway for takeoff, I felt convicted. Even after spending several days reaching out to the hurting, the poor, and the anguished, I had let my heart grow a little bit hard.

But Ricky showed me that the compassion he is known for is always in season and knows no limit. In other words, he walks the talk. Just as God never closes His eyes, we should keep our eyes open in order that God can help us go beyond the limits of our human frailties.

Satan is always trying to rob us of these moments of availability. He'll rob us by saying: "You're tired, you need your rest." "You're busy." "Of course you'd like to help, but you just don't have time."

"Take a look at your watch. If you get involved, you'll miss your next appointment."

But on the way home, I remembered a story that Sami Dagher had shared with me, a story that speaks powerfully of how we can step beyond the limits and be mightily used by Him when we reach out to others.

THE BIG FISH

In the late seventies, Sami Dagher woke up in the middle of the night from a restless sleep, troubled in his spirit. Lebanon was in the midst of that vicious civil war between the Muslim PLO and the Lebanese Christians. "Lord," he prayed, "give me an opportunity to share my faith with somebody today."

Later that morning, Sami got in his Volkswagen microbus, heading to his office. As Sami drove through the narrow and crowded streets of Beirut, he noticed a strange sight—a Syrian army officer hitchhiking. Sami couldn't remember seeing a Syrian officer hitchhiking in Lebanon before, and for good reason—he was as likely to catch a bullet as he was a ride. At this stage in the Lebanese civil war, Syria had taken the side of the PLO (later they switched), funneling guns and ammunition to the guerrillas. They came in later as reputed peacekeepers; in reality, they simply hoped to get a piece of Sami's beloved Lebanon.

Sami saw the soldier and immediately became indignant. *No way would I ever give him a ride,* Sami thought. *Why don't those Syrians leave us alone? They've caused enough trouble.*

As Sami drove past the soldier, something inside made him slow down. He remembered his restless sleep and his prayer in the middle of the night: "Lord, give me an opportunity to share my faith with somebody today."

Ah, a big fish, Sami thought, as he looked into the rearview mirror. *God is giving me a big fish.*

Sami turned his van around and pulled off on the gravel embankment, stopping just in front of the Syrian officer. At first the soldier was understandably wary, but he saw Sami's warm expression and climbed into the van.

"Where are you headed?" Sami asked.

The officer told him, and though he was headed in a slightly different direction from where Sami planned to go, Sami said, "I'll take you there."

Sami had his big fish on the hook.

Sami didn't waste any time engaging the man in conversation, and quickly got to the subject weighing most heavily on his heart. As he neared the destination, he noticed that it was getting close to the noon hour. Sami didn't feel that he had gotten to say all he had to say—he needed more time to present the gospel. "Have you had lunch?" he asked the officer.

"No."

"You would honor my home with your presence if you would have lunch with me," he said.

The Syrian officer's forehead wrinkled up like a well-worn map. It was surprising enough that a Lebanese Christian would give him a ride. But lunch?

Sami encouraged him.

The Syrian smiled in spite of himself. "OK, I'll come," he said.

Sami's heart leaped. But he quickly realized that there was no time to notify his wife, Joy. He stopped at a roadside grill along the way and bought a roasted chicken.

At home, Sami's wife cheerfully prepared a typical Lebanese meal—charcoal chicken (Beirut is home to the best-cooked chicken in the world) and flat pita bread with some fresh raw vegetables. Sami kept serving generous portions of chicken to the Syrian officer; the longer the man ate, the longer Sami had to tell him about what Christ had done for him. Sami fed his guest every morsel of chicken to keep him occupied, wondering all the while if anything he was saying was sinking in. When the chicken was gone, the man pushed back from the table and said, "Thank you, I must be on my way."

The officer had shown no emotion as Sami shared the gospel. He didn't seem angry, but neither did he seem particularly interested. He just listened politely. Sami got up, dismayed, but drove the man to where he needed to go and waved good-bye.

Sami never saw him again. He felt that perhaps he had failed; maybe he should have bought two chickens! Or maybe he had just taken the wrong approach. Regardless of the lack of response, Sami was thankful that God had given him an opportunity to share his faith just as he had prayed.

THE REST OF THE STORY

Sami wanted the Syrian officer to get on his knees immediately and ask Christ to come into his life, but God had other plans.

Paul Harvey is famous for hanging his audience in suspense as he tells his behind-the-scene stories. He keeps you guessing until the fabulous wrap, "And now the rest of the story."

"The rest of this story" for Sami Dagher and the Syrian soldier is remarkable. To live beyond the limits is to be on God's timetable. Often that means we must be patient.

Several years after Sami offered a ride and a chicken lunch to the Syrian officer, a young Christian dentist living in Damascus decided to open his own clinic. Before anyone was allowed to do that, however, the Syrian socialist government required several years of government service. The young dentist was assigned to a little mud village in the eastern district, near the Iraqi border. He began using every opportunity to tell his patients about the love of Jesus Christ. After all, he reasoned, in the dentist's chair they were certainly a captive audience, and they couldn't very well argue back when he had his hands and instruments in their mouths!

There are safer places in the world to share your faith in Christ than in Syria. Word soon spread among the villagers about the Christian dentist in their midst. When it became clear that the young dentist would neither renounce his faith nor stop talking about it, the local religious leaders decided to punish him.

There was just one problem. Since the dentist worked for the government, he was technically a government employee. You can't go out and harm a government employee and get away with it, so the religious leaders approached the military police, urging them to bring charges against this man so they could legitimize their persecution.

The officer in charge was obligated to interrogate the dentist. For you to understand what happened next, you must completely erase any notion of *interrogation* that you may have from watching police shows on television. In Syria, interrogation can be worse than death.

The young dentist was prepared for interrogation by being "softened up," which meant they would whip him, beat him, kick him, and then begin asking questions.

"Who are you?" the soldiers demanded, and the dentist gave them his name.

"Where are you from?"

"Damascus."

"What are you?"

"I'm a Christian. I belong to the Church of Damascus."

The Syrian officer leading the interrogation immediately shouted, "Stop!" and ordered every military man out of the room. The dentist swallowed hard.

This man's going to kill me, he thought, *and there won't be any witnesses.*

When the room was cleared, the officer leaned over his chair and asked, "Do you know a man in Beirut by the name of Sami Dagher?"

The young man did know Sami because Sami had preached in

his church, but how in the world could this officer know Sami. *Oh, no, the dentist gulped. What has Sami done now? And what will happen to me since I know him?*

As a believer, the dentist knew he couldn't lie, so with a hushed reluctance he looked at his interrogator. "Yes, I know Sami Dagher."

"If you know Sami Dagher of Beirut," the officer stood tall, "you're free to go and continue your work."

The dentist let out a sigh of shocked relief as the officer told him how, several years earlier, Sami Dagher had picked him up and given him a chicken for lunch. During that lunch, the officer recounted, Sami had told him the "most wonderful" story that he had ever heard in his life; the story of a Savior who came out of heaven to this earth to die for the sins of this world. If he would believe in this Savior, his own wrongdoings could be forgiven.

"I've had a sweet taste in my mouth ever since," he told the young dentist. "I have never forgotten his words."

The Syrian officer never gave the dentist any indication that he had become a Christian, but because of Sami's faithfulness and obedience, even to his enemy, that officer spared the young dentist. Several years earlier, when Sami had prayed for the opportunity to share his faith, he never dreamed that sharing a chicken with a Syrian officer would spare the life and ministry of a fellow believer two years later. This is what is meant by living beyond the limits. God can use even an ordinary act of providing a chicken lunch to accomplish His will. He can use you if you are willing.

God's Outposts

When I think of Sami's story, I'm reminded of Galatians 6:10: "*As we have opportunity, let us do good to all people*" (NIV).

If we want to become the type of people that God can use any time, anywhere, any place, we must offer ourselves, our homes, our kitchens, and our living rooms as outposts for the kingdom of God, places where He can bring people together. This is often where people may play a strategic role in the advancement of God's work on earth.

If Sami had been rude, honked his horn, and shook his fist at the Syrian, that young dentist might be dead. Sami chose to live beyond the limitations of biased feelings. Thirty minutes of kindness and a buck-fifty chicken saved a man's life! This demonstrates the radical importance that hospitality can have when it is offered in Christ's name. The Bible tells us, *"Offer hospitality to one another . . . so that in all things God may be praised"* (1 Peter 4:9, 11 NIV). Sami took what God had given him—an old van, a small apartment, and a chicken—and trusted God to do something great.

Today, God's kingdom is being built over backyard fences: through a cup of coffee shared with a hurting neighbor, through an encouraging word offered on the Ford assembly line in Detroit, through a businessman taking a colleague out to lunch in New York, or through Ricky Skaggs stopping to help a woman in tears in a foreign country. Whatever we have—our cars, our homes, our churches—our challenge is to offer everything up as an outpost for God's kingdom, a place where God can advance His work through you.

When we walk in sync with God, He can take even our worst experiences—coming from a dysfunctional home, losing a parent at a young age, having an unfortunate background—and use them for His good.

All of us can be guilty of excusing our problems. But there is no excuse to justify our sinful behavior. We want to point the finger to someone else or another set of circumstances and lay the blame there. We live in a decaying society where people refuse to take responsibility for their own actions.

Think about Joseph, who was sold into slavery by his brothers. He didn't let bitterness consume him. He allowed God to work this out for good in his life and rose to become the second most powerful man in all the land. His brothers meant his enslavement for evil, but God meant it—and used it—for good.

A close friend of mine, Greg Laurie, is pastor of one of the most flourishing churches in southern California. His mother was married seven times, and to this day he doesn't know who his biological father is. Seven times, in the course of Greg's childhood, he came home from school and heard his mom say, "Sorry, honey, I found a new man and we're moving."

At age seventeen, Greg heard a pastor from Calvary Chapel, Costa Mesa, present the gospel, and he gave his heart to Christ. Today, Greg pastors the eighth largest church in the United States. He's a successful author and evangelist (drawing people to some of the largest crusades in our country today), and he has found how to take the pain of his past and his experiences as a child and surrender them to God. Greg doesn't make excuses; on the contrary, by walking with God he uses his experiences in life to help others who suffer from painful pasts.

You can play a role that nobody else can. It's your choice. Don't get out of step by focusing on your own personal difficulties and misfortunes. Keep your eyes and thoughts on the Lord so that your spirit will be sensitive to His leading.

Don't let your past cause vibrations that shake you out of God's will. Since God can obviously use even a chicken, you can choose to use everything God has allowed in your life to live beyond what you thought was impossible.

You'll be amazed at how God will guide and direct your path. We are told in the Scriptures to *"Be wise in the way you act toward outsiders; make the most of every opportunity. Let your conversation be always full of grace, seasoned with salt, so that you may know how to answer everyone"* (Col. 4:5–6 NIV).

G OD CAN AND DOES use people. God will use us if we'll let Him. One of the more moving lessons for me in my travels has been the understanding that God also uses situations. I've found myself in the midst of some heartbreaking circumstances— witnessing the effects of civil war, ethnic cleansing, drought, flooding, virtually every catastrophe possible it seems. But I have yet to come across one in which God couldn't be glorified in some way.

That's true even of death.

A few years ago, I was in Bosnia with Samaritan's Purse shortly after the signing of the Dayton Peace Accord. This agreement stated that some of the villages taken over by the Serbs had to be returned to the Muslims and Croats. The Serbs responded by returning "villages" that bore only a slight resemblance to the homelands once inhabited by the original Muslim and Croatian residents. Many of these small towns had been ripped to shreds and pillaged unmercifully. Samaritan's Purse was there to help put the lives of the villagers back together.

That's how I found myself in the tiny, predominantly Muslim village of Hadzici, not far from where the Sarajevo Winter Olympics had been held. A local principal was giving me a tour of the school, and one of my team members, Duane Gaylord, whispered, "Ask the principal to show you the gymnasium." Duane wanted to make sure I saw it because he had heard that this was going to be investigated by the UN as a war-crime site.

We walked through rubble as the principal pointed to the gym. "They call it *Auschwitz*," he explained, for reasons that you'll come to know about shortly.

We walked down a flight of steps and went through a door where the glass had been blown out. There was at least an inch of standing water in the hallway, and I was sickened by the musty smell of death as we approached the gym. The principal pointed out a young boy who was kicking his soccer ball against a wall marked by bullet holes. "He's been here most of the day and keeps coming back," the principal said.

"What's his story?" I asked.

I learned that by the time little Laris Bajus was nine years old, his hometown of Hadzici was caught in the vicious war between Serbs, Muslims, and Croats. It was not a fair war. From the beginning, the Serbs had plenty of guns. The Muslims and Croats had very little, and in some cases virtually nothing, with which to defend themselves. Little villages like Hadzici fell instantly and soon experienced the horror of "ethnic cleansing." The Muslims—and that included Laris's family—were treated in ways not seen since Nazi Germany. The Serbs violated virtually every aspect of the Geneva convention, which basically wrote the rules for how combatants and noncombatants are to be treated during a war.

The Serb army committed acts of unbelievable atrocity and encouraged rape. The rationale was that if non-Serb soldiers heard that their wives, daughters, and mothers were being molested while they were away in the trenches, they would abandon their posts and run home to protect their loved ones. Thus rape became a deplorable weapon designed to demoralize enemy troops.

War doesn't get much uglier. Non-Serb civilians were subjected to electrode shocks, body mutilation, upside-down hanging, and every hellish act thinkable. If demons were allowed to run wild, they couldn't have got any more creative than the army that occupied Laris's village.

One day, Serb soldiers rounded up Laris's father and a number of other men. Laris watched his father being shoved around, and he felt his legs grow weak when he saw the horrible fear darkening his mother's eyes as she watched. The men were led at gunpoint outside the village. Several hours later, the soldiers returned, but Laris's father and the other men did not.

As the weather turned cold, the soldiers moved their dirty work inside. They chose the school gym where Laris had spent some of the best hours of his life playing sports and attending classes. Instead of being the hub of community life, as it once was, the gym soon became a sepulchre of death. Locals began to refer to it as "Auschwitz."

The Serb soldiers would round up Croats, Muslims, and other non-Serbs and herd them into the gym. Later corpses were carried out. Children who dared to venture close enough to the gym's outside walls heard cries of pain, pleas for mercy, and then sharp bursts of gunfire and bloodcurdling screams.

Muslims began fleeing the village, but the Serbs had thought ahead and prepared the escape route by mining the mountain trails. The chilling stories of legless citizens (people whose lower limbs had been blown off by land mines) kept many of the refugees off the trails. Instead, they risked crossing open pastures, where they were prime targets for sniper fire.

In the winter, snow up to seven feet deep removed the danger of the land mines, but temperatures that plummeted thirty to forty degrees below zero made travel over the mountains perilous, especially for mothers with small children. Even so, many Muslims braved the dangerous trek, choosing almost certain frostbite and starvation over torture and execution.

The villagers of Hadzici kept thinking life would eventually get better. *Surely the West will intervene and stop this,* they thought. A number of Muslim families—including Laris and his mother— tried to hang on rather than risk the dangerous flight over the mountains. But life didn't get better, and eventually, Laris's worst nightmare came true when soldiers knocked down his front door and dragged his mother to "Auschwitz."

Laris never saw her again.

Like so many young Bosnian children, Laris was now an orphan. There was no professional counseling, no grief management, no special programs in which Laris might voice his pain and find relief. There was not even a graveside he might visit to pay his last respects to his mother or father. There was no announcement of their passing or acknowledgment of their contribution, just the soul-numbing realization that at nine years old he was on his own.

HE WON'T LEAVE IT

Several months later, the Dayton Peace Accord directed that Hadzici be redrawn as a Muslim territory, and the Serbs were forced to leave per the agreement. Caught off guard, the Serbs did their best to quickly clean up "Auschwitz." Executions are a crude business, and the Serbs weren't nearly done by the time French troops arrived and ordered them to evacuate. The Serbs stalled.

"We'll leave the rest of the town," they said, "but we'll keep the gym for now."

"No," the French ordered. They knew what was inside the gym and immediately called for reinforcements. "If you don't evacu- ate immediately," the French warned the Serbs, "we're going to open fire."

The Serbs blinked. In the days before they finally left, they stripped the school and every Muslim home of anything even remotely valuable. They removed every window glass, tore off roof tiles, and took basketball backboards from the goalposts. They even carted away the porcelain toilets. French soldiers found that the

Serbs had also unbolted several iron radiators, but apparently found them too heavy to move and left them just a few inches away from where they had been.

What the Serbs did leave behind was a ghastly horror. Blood spatters, matted and twisted hair, and mangled bodies sickened the stomachs of the French soldiers who occupied the gym. The executions and tortures had created what looked like a human parts factory.

The telltale signs of human debris made it relatively clear what had transpired. The walls and the floor of the gymnasium were pockmarked by bullet holes. The bloodstains told a vivid story—this was where the villagers had been lined up and systematically shot.

Laris didn't have a clue where his parents' bodies were, but at least he knew where his mother had died. Within these four walls, he had discovered the last place on earth that her precious body had stood of its own accord, waiting to meet the bullets that would bring her life to a tragic and premature end.

As soon as Laris was free to roam about the village, he headed straight for the gymnasium. He spent hours there, kicking an old soccer ball against the very walls that marked his mother's death. The still-visible bullet holes were a heart-wrenching reminder of what had taken place there. I wondered if Laris kicked the old tattered ball in anger, perhaps imagining he was getting back at the Serbs.

"I think he must feel closer to his mother in here," the principal explained.

I hurt for this boy. I became angry at the people who caused such turmoil and pain for Laris's family and others. It made me want to fight back, but I knew that to bring glory to God and go beyond human limits we must reach out in love in Christ's name.

The Gut-Level Realities of Life

Spending time with Laris reminded me of how death points us back to the gut-level realities of life. I love to hunt, but there's something startling that occurs to every hunter. It is a process that can still cause you to pause and consider what you're doing.

Many times I have put the crosshairs of my rifle sight on the neck and shoulder of a moose, caribou, or deer—and more often than not, I've let the animal go. These are strong animals; their poetic motion is wonderfully complemented by brute strength. But when you know you're there to hunt and bring them down, your heart races, you steady your hand, and fire. The animal stumbles. You watch it fall. Quickly, you load another round and approach cautiously—many hunters have been killed or seriously maimed by a wounded animal.

As a hunter, you have to clean the animal quickly or the meat will spoil. As soon as possible, I take my knife, cut open the animal, and pull out the heart, intestines, stomach, and lungs. The warm blood on my hands reminds me that just a few moments ago this animal was standing in front of me, alive, and now I have my hands in its body.

Hunters and farmers understand the mystery of life and death. One minute you're here, the next minute you're gone.

It's a lesson we all need to learn. Ultimately, it doesn't matter how sensibly you eat or how meticulously you plan your diet; you can even work out at the gym three hours a day. Even so, eventually, you're going to die. So be ready.

As King Solomon said, *"To everything there is a season, a time for every purpose under heaven: a time to be born, and a time to die"* (Eccl. 3:1–2).

LIVING WITH DEATH

Facing death—not only our own passing, but the passing of our loved ones—is one of the most difficult parts of life. In modern North America, death has been largely removed from our daily experience and hidden away behind the closed doors of hospital rooms and hospices. Sudden death may haunt those entrapped in violent, inner-city neighborhoods, but it's extremely rare for most of us actually to see a real death occur. Sure, we see countless deaths on television, but when death visits someone we actually know, we're caught off guard. And like Laris, we create our own ways to deal with our pain and suffering.

A well-known recording artist and friend of mine watched his mother try to handle the death of her husband in a different way. She spent entire days at her husband's graveside talking to him.

Finally, my friend told his mother, "Mama, if you wanna sit here for hours talking to Daddy, you might get an answer, but it ain't gonna be from God, and it ain't gonna be from Daddy. He's not here anymore; he's in heaven."

Death can be so painful that we even cling to a six-foot patch of dirt that holds the remains of our loved one's body.

I think that's what Laris was doing. As a young Muslim, he had no assurance about the eternal state of his parents. As a young child, death had perhaps become more real to him than life itself. If he couldn't go to his mom, at least he could go to the place where she was killed. And who could blame him?

We live in a fallen world. For the believer, though, death is the vehicle that God uses to take our souls from earth to heaven and be ushered into His eternal presence. Our confidence is not in the grave. As believers, when we die, we're not saying, "Good-bye, forever." We're saying merely, "See you later."

If we want to walk in sync with God, we have to realize that death is a part of life—not only our death, but the deaths of our mentors, relatives, and friends. For those who have not accepted Christ's work on the cross as redemption for their sins, their souls are lost for eternity.

But you see, God has a plan. It is not God's will to take away life—instead He has provided a way of escape. Second Samuel 14:14 says: *"But God does not take away life; instead, he devises ways so that a banished person may not remain estranged from him"* (NIV).

What are God's ways? John 3:16 says, *"For God so loved the world that He gave His only begotten Son, that whoever believes in Him should not perish but have everlasting life."*

Being religious will not save us. *"If we say that we have no sin, we deceive ourselves, and the truth is not in us. If we confess our sins, He is faithful and just to forgive us our sins and to cleanse us from all unrighteousness"* (1 John 1:8–9). We must choose to receive Christ. Our good works will not save us. The Bible says, *"By grace you have been saved through faith, and . . . not of works, lest anyone should boast"* (Eph. 2:8–9).

The only way we will ever truly live a life beyond human limits is when we come into a full and right relationship with His Son, Jesus Christ. This is the beginning. If we don't have this relationship, nothing else is going to matter.

ONE THING IN COMMON

In 1996 my mother and father were jointly awarded the Congressional Medal of Honor, our nation's highest award given to civilians. Some of the most powerful people in our country—the speaker of the house, the senate majority leader, members of the Supreme Court, and military leaders—gathered to honor my parents in our nation's Capitol.

After the award was presented, my father was asked to respond to the distinguished dignitaries who had gathered in the Capitol Rotunda. This section of the Capitol is ringed with statues of our nation's most notable forefathers, including George Washington, Thomas Jefferson, and Abraham Lincoln.

My father, ironically enough, stood just in front of Ulysses S. Grant. As a Southerner, his relatives might have had something to say about that, but Daddy diplomatically passed up the opportunity

Dr. Steve Duncan in Angola in 1984.

Dennis Agajanian and Michael W. Smith play and sing for a group of kids on the cancer ward at the world's largest children's hospital in Soweto, South Africa, in 1997.

Mary Damron helps me give away gifts to children in General Hospital in Bosnia in 1995.

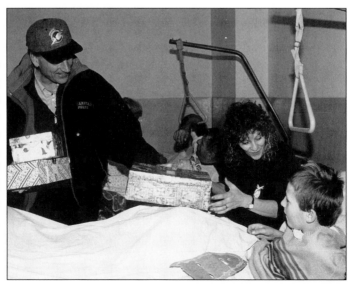

Sami Dagher (left) and I review the remains of this young Palestinian man's home in the Shatila Refugee Camp on the outskirts of Beirut, Lebanon, in 1982.

The first opportunity my father and I had to preach together was in Saskatoon, Saskatchewan, in 1995.

Ricky Skaggs and his wife, Sharon White Skaggs, perform in a bombed-out sports arena in Bihác, Bosnia, in 1995.

Dennis Agajanian and Ricky and Sharon Skaggs share their tremendous talents with children inside Bosnia during Christmas of 1995.

My friend Commander Mohammed with his prize cow in 1996.

My sister Anne Graham Lotz, one of the great speakers in America today. She has a real sense of style and class.

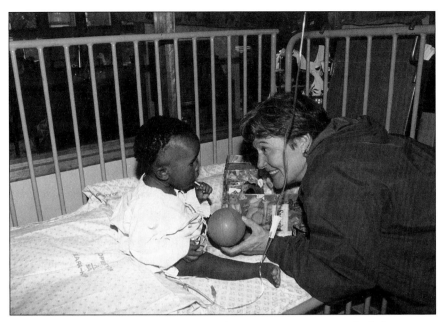

My wife, Jane Austin, is able to travel with me on occasion. Here she helps deliver Christmas gifts to sick children in South Africa in 1997.

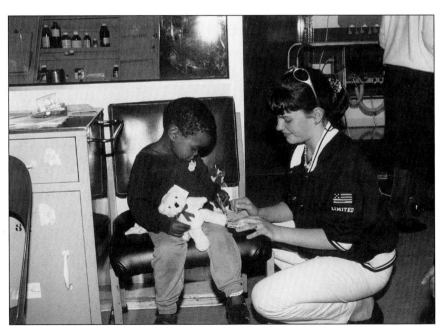

One of the greatest opportunities I have as a father is being able to take my children on trips from time to time. My daughter, Cissie, accompanied me in 1997 to Africa, where she helped distribute gifts to children in one of the large hospitals.

My mother, Ruth Bell Graham, with Dr. Eleanor Soltau in 1993. They were in school together in North Korea before World War II and later at Wheaton College. Dr. Soltau was accidentally burned to death at age eighty in the fall of 1997 while still ministering to her beloved Bedouin friends in the desert of northern Jordan.

Dr. Eleanor Soltau (left) with Aileen Coleman in front of Mafraq Hospital in northern Jordan in the late 1960s.

Dr. Richard
Furman on our
first medical
mission trip to
Papua New
Guinea in 1977.

Andy
Meakins,
TEAR Fund
representative,
with his wife
in Ethiopia—
1988.

Dr. Robert
Foster (right)
with one of
his beloved
African
pastors in
Angola
in 1992.

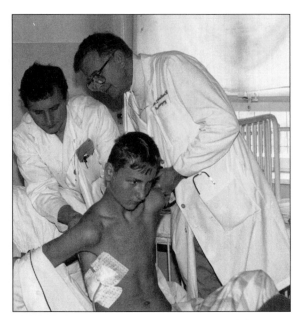

*Dr. Mel Cheatham (right) with Dr. Josip (left)
examining a young boy who had been wounded
during the fighting in Zenica, Bosnia, in 1993.*

*Dr. Mel Cheatham (left) and his wife, Sylvia, (right) with one of the French UN
peacekeepers in Bosnia in 1993.*

and instead referred to something else that moved me and the assembled leaders very deeply.

"All of the statues in this room, every last one of them, have something in common," Daddy said, sweeping the room with his arm.

My father paused and then said, "Each one of them is dead."

Being a successful Civil War general doesn't excuse you from death. Just because you opened up the West with an explorer's courage doesn't mean you won't be buried in it. Walking among these statues, you see people who have done it all—Will Rogers, who built a career out of making people laugh; Frances Willard, a strong woman from Illinois who led the Temperance movement; inventors, explorers, educators, scholars, government leaders, you name it—yet not one of them lived beyond his or her appointed time. Regardless of what you achieve, how much money you earn, or how much knowledge you attain, you're going to die.

Death, for the believer, is really an exchange of our earthly dwelling for a heavenly home. *"But our citizenship is in heaven. And we eagerly await a Savior from there, the Lord Jesus Christ, who, by the power that enables him to bring everything under his control, will transform our lowly bodies so that they will be like his glorious body"* (Phil. 3:20–21 NIV). Here on earth we choose our destiny. In death we realize the result of our choice—everlasting joy in heaven or eternal torment in hell. Where will you spend *forever?*

FIRST THINGS FIRST

When you think of it, none of us know the hour of our deaths any more than a buck does sprinting through the woods. Our bullet might be cancer, AIDS, a stroke, heart disease, an automobile accident. But we do know this: It's coming—we just don't know when.

I have a friend who was the first to break the land-speed record, traveling over 700 miles an hour in a rocket car. (Talk about exceeding the limit!) As a Hollywood stunt man, he spends three to four hours a day building up his body to withstand the rigors of his profession. Imagine where we'd be if we spent as much time building our souls as we do building our bodies.

We don't have to guess what it would be like to spend more time preparing our souls than we do our bodies. The apostle Paul provided us with a wonderful example, and this was his conclusion:

> *Do you not know that in a race all the runners run, but only one gets the prize? Run in such a way as to get the prize. Everyone who competes in the games goes into strict training. They do it to get a crown that will not last; but we do it to get a crown that will last forever. Therefore I do not run like a man running aimlessly; I do not fight like a man beating the air. No, I beat my body and make it my slave so that after I have preached to others, I myself will not be disqualified for the prize.* (1 Cor. 9:24–27 NIV)

Will your death be a doorway to peace, or a portal of fear? Jesus said, *"I am the resurrection and the life. He who believes in Me, though he may die, he shall live"* (John 11:25).

COMMANDER MOHAMMED

W AKING TO THE MORNING NEWS these days is dismal. Another war is breaking out in a foreign land. Floods are filling the heartland. Earthquakes and mudslides threaten the West Coast. El Niño is coming again.

And this is in addition to the troubles in our own neighborhoods and churches—a young mother has given birth to a disabled baby; an elderly woman has just buried her husband; a young boy has gunned down teenagers on school property; cancer has taken another precious life.

The heartache seems endless. In fact, it can be so monumental that we sometimes want to just walk away. "It's too much to handle," we insist. "I can't comfort everyone in their need, so maybe I shouldn't try to help anyone."

Friends, that is a lie from the pit of hell. We will never be able to meet everyone's needs, but we have to start somewhere.

Samaritan's Purse is faced with bad news almost daily. Our fax machines and electronic mailboxes overflow with bulletins from missionaries and national Christians who are bombarded with countless trials and tribulations. They cry out for help. We believe that God has called us to respond to His people with His endless resources. And when God calls, He provides.

One such call came from the troubled country of Bosnia—a very difficult country in which to work. The mountainous terrain surrounding many of its small villages makes relief work difficult, at best. Even worse, Bosnia's many different ethnic groups have been spilling each other's blood for centuries. Working in Bosnia is complex. When you enter a country that has the fragmentation of a jigsaw puzzle, how do you begin to put the pieces back together?

We couldn't help everyone, so we chose Laris Bajus's hometown — Hadzici. There were other places we could have gone, but I believe that sometimes you just need to get started right where you are. And God had placed us in this little village. So we rolled up our sleeves and went to work.

Wherever we go, we find the needs so great. We can't possibly bring in enough doctors, so the physicians must prioritize whom they can see. This is called medical triage, and it's also practiced during major catastrophes. Physicians make decisions based on patient condition, available equipment, and odds of successful recovery.

While some Christians are thrown out of sync with God through apathy, we can also be thrown out of sync by becoming overwhelmed by *every* opportunity. It breaks our hearts to pass by some needs in order to help with others, but sometimes we have no other choice. What gives us assurance is in knowing that God is guiding our every step. He walks through the open doors before we even arrive.

One look at the village of Hadzici was enough to tell me that prioritizing the reconstruction there wouldn't be an easy task, so we did what doctors do: We performed "village triage." We decided to look for the families that were the worst off and help them first.

We developed a plan to take homes whose roofs had been destroyed and to put at least the shell back together. If we could put new roofs on the houses, the people could repair the walls and replace the windows and the furniture. With a roof, at the very least the people could keep dry and warm and preserve their strength to face the severe winter cold and the daunting task of starting their lives all over again.

As soon as we were able to do that for one family, we'd go to the next family on our list, helping as many as we could. Instead of allowing ourselves to be overwhelmed with despair (*It's too much!*), we committed ourselves to achievable tasks.

It became clear that one success story could provide the jolt needed to get people moving again. Families would walk by the once bombed-out house, see the new roof, and say to each other, "We ought to go back to the ruins of our old house, shovel out the debris, and maybe we can start over too."

It sounds simplistic, but it's true: By simply repairing a roof, we knew God could use this act of kindness in His name as the inspiration to move the entire Muslim village, making a tremendous impact for the gospel.

The same thing can happen in your community. Caring is infectious. By being a volunteer or by getting involved with someone who is less fortunate than you, you can have an impact that can change your community. God can use you as the catalyst to change hearts, attitudes, and perceptions.

I remember Samaritan Purse founder Bob Pierce telling me, "Buddy, you can't help everybody, but you can help a few. It's that few that God will hold us accountable for."

That's right. Once people see you meeting a need, they'll be challenged to become involved as well. The important thing is to get started and watch God open up avenues that will take your life beyond what you ever dreamed possible.

THE SOLDIER AND HIS COW

One of the first houses that we selected to work on belonged to an old war hero named Mohammed, a commander in the Bosnian army who was renowned for recapturing huge chunks of Bosnia during the war. Mohammed, a fifty-year-old Muslim, was a proud man. His chiseled features seemed a symbol of his noble determination to survive. His thinning brown hair was highlighted with wisps of gray, and his blue eyes were so fierce that they appeared as though they could cut through steel.

Because of his war exploits, Mohammed was a celebrated figure in Bosnia, though his heroism had come at a tremendous personal cost. During one battle, Mohammed stepped on one of Bosnia's reportedly two million land mines and lost both his legs. On top of this debilitating injury, Mohammed was faced with another great personal loss. His son was killed shortly after Mohammed lost his legs, leaving behind a wife and three children.

Mohammed's fame would be similar to a Sergeant York from World War I or Colonel Tex Hill, the famed Flying Tiger ace from World War II. But this war hero didn't even receive a pension from the government he had served. Though he had sacrificed two legs and the life of his son on behalf of his country, his government couldn't lift a finger to help him. Bosnia was just too poor.

I liked Commander Mohammed from the moment I saw him. He didn't let his injury keep him from standing erect in self-confidence, sticking his chest out, and holding his head high, while hobbling on crutches with his two crude prosthetic legs! He's a tough man, and if he thought you pitied him he would just as soon push you down as shake your hand.

Even though he is crippled, in his own mind Mohammed is still a military officer, and he bears the dignity and stature of the best of them. I've seen guys who were wounded in war, and they let themselves slide. They grow sloppy about their appearance and spend their days feeling sorry for themselves; Mohammed wasn't the type of man who would let that happen.

Yet this proud and determined double amputee looked out at me from a house without windows in a kitchen that had no roof. He carried a heavy load. Because his son had been killed, he had to care for his daughter-in-law and her three children. He didn't have time to cry over his war wounds. He had a large family to feed.

Life on a farm in the Bosnian mountains isn't easy. Life on a farm that has been looted and plundered is even more difficult. But life as a double amputee on a Bosnian *mountain* farm that is looted and blown up is almost unimaginable.

How in the world can he plow his field and harvest his crop while sitting in a wheelchair or hobbling on his crutches? I wondered, as I looked at the mountains around him.

Our village triage operation went to work, and we had the privilege of putting a roof on Commander Mohammed's house. Once it was finished I went back to see it, and Mohammed proudly showed me the good workmanship that would keep his family dry. I noticed that he still didn't have any windows, so we decided to install some on the second floor, where he could frame in a couple of rooms to keep the cold winds and snow away from his family.

Still, there was the matter of the mountainous farm and Mohammed's crutches, so I asked him, "How are you going to survive the winter?"

Tears brimmed the eyes of this tough, battle-hardened commander. "I don't know," he said. "If I had a cow, we would have some butter, cheese, and milk for the grandchildren. Maybe then we could make it."

I was moved by Mohammed's sense of responsibility. Though living in a situation that would have cast weaker men into despair and self-pity, Mohammed was focused on his family's dependency on him. I could envision him going weeks without food, saving the few remnants for the tiny, hungry mouths of his grandchildren. He wasn't seeking a handout. He just thoughtfully answered, "If I only had a cow . . ."

I live in Boone, North Carolina, and have plenty of cows for neighbors. As a matter of fact, they come right through the fence and into my yard, uninvited, all the time! A single cow really doesn't mean that much here in North America. If anything, cows can be a real nuisance—especially when the fence is down.

However, in Bosnia a single cow can mean the difference between life and death; between a bountiful winter or a hungry winter.

As I left the commander that day, I told Kent Elliott, our Samaritan's Purse country director at the time, "I'm personally going to buy Mohammed a cow." At Samaritan's Purse we do lots of projects, but occasionally I like to do a few things on my own. I learned this from my parents. Growing up, my mother and father maintained a Family Help Fund, something that would be used to help others above and beyond the tithe. My parents would teach us kids to set aside a little extra money and let it accumulate. Sometimes the fund would grow to as much as $1,000. Times came where a family in our community would be in need due to a father losing a job, or a family home being burned to the ground, or someone with medical bills that couldn't be paid. We would be able to give this few hundred dollars, or more, to those in need. It was a wonderful lesson growing up.

Following this example, Jane Austin and I have tried to teach our children about the privilege of helping those less fortunate. I believe in tithing, but I also believe in giving gifts above the tithe. I thought that Mohammed's situation presented my family with a wonderful opportunity. We couldn't afford to buy a cow for every family in Bosnia, but we could manage one milk cow for Mohammed. Within a few weeks, Kent delivered the cow to Commander Mohammed.

Later that year, I was able to return to Mohammed's village for a visit. It has been said that the eyes are the windows to the soul. That certainly was the case with Mohammed as I saw the reflection of a renewed hope and an increased sense of pride when he showed me that cow. Now, Mohammed could get his family through the long, hard winter.

And, boy, did he take care of that cow! That was one fat animal, and believe me, it was living as high as a cow can live grazing from the fertile Bosnian hills. Mohammed kept it in the bottom portion of his house, treating that "pet" almost like a child. His family depended on that cow, and he wasn't about to let anything happen to it.

"You Christians,
You're the Only Ones Who Help"

To my Muslim friends, Westerners are seen as decadent, imperialistic, immoral drunkards. Many of their images of the typical Westerner come from television trash talk shows and movies that portray sex and violence.

Because I'm fully aware of this perception, it was particularly meaningful to me when Mohammed wiped a tear from his eye and said, "You Christians, you're the only ones who help us."

I don't know if Mohammed will ever come to know Jesus Christ as his personal Lord and Savior. I have shared with him my faith and prayed with him, but he must choose for himself. One thing I know, there is at least one family that will be told that some gifts given in the name of Jesus Christ made a difference in their lives one bleak winter.

This wasn't the first time I had heard this sentiment, by the way. In the early part of the war, before I met Mohammed, I traveled on a homemade ferry across the Slava river to a little town called Orasje. We took truckloads of food into a besieged city, and we set up a little food kitchen. The imam (a Muslim spiritual leader) took me aside one day, and with gratitude written all over his face, told me exactly the same thing: "You Christians are the only ones who are helping." Can't you just see God smiling? (And the devil frowning!)

The Key of Kindness

I can't imagine anyone being more frustrated than the devil. Think about it. He unleashes the most demonic acts of cruelty, hatred, and division, and he uses people to carry out his atrocities. The Serbs treated the Muslims with less compassion than they would treat a dog. Hadzici was virtually destroyed, pillaged right down to the porcelain toilets.

Just when Satan thought he had triumphed, Christians stood and said, "Satan, you can't have Bosnia. In Christ's name, we're going into Bosnia, we're going to tend to the sick, we're going to care for the dying, and we're going to reach out to the lost. We will love them, help rebuild their towns, give them food, and do whatever it takes to bring the gospel of Jesus Christ to Bosnia."

What did these Christians ask in return? Nothing. You see, when human cruelty reaches its zenith, that's when we as Christians need to go on the offensive. How? By looking for the need and being willing to do something about it. Telling them the good news of a God who loves us, who sent His Son to die for us.

The devil is warring against all people, trying to turn them away from the only One who can truly save them from their sins—Jesus Christ—who says: *"I am the door. If anyone enters by Me, he will be saved, and will go in and out and find pasture. The thief does not come except to steal, and to kill, and to destroy. I have come that they may have life, and that they may have it more abundantly"* (John 10:9–10). Kindness is often the key that will unlock people's hearts, motivating them to consider the claims of the Savior.

OVERCOMING EVIL WITH GOOD

For many years, government leaders have tried to focus our nation on humanitarian efforts; from John F. Kennedy's "Ask what you can do for your country" to General Colin Powell's calling Americans to volunteerism. But it shouldn't take political leaders to motivate us to get involved. We should be motivated because of what Christ has done for us. *"But whoever has this world's goods, and sees his brother in need, and shuts up his heart from him, how does the love of God abide in him?"* (1 John 3:17).

The same principle that we employed in Bosnia will work in your neighborhood. Maybe a family is rocked by unemployment; perhaps there's been a local tragedy, a group of teenagers killed or seriously injured in an automobile accident; maybe a major business is laying off hundreds of workers.

In these dark situations, God wants to use you to shine the message of hope into people's hearts—but for that message to be heard, it takes more than just words. You've got to get involved. Words without action are cheap. The early Christians knew this. The apostle John told them: *"Let us not love in word or in tongue, but in deed and in truth"* (1 John 3:18).

With the hope, generosity, and reconciling love of the gospel of Jesus Christ, these practical acts of compassion can carry a profound message—as they did in Hadzici.

Before Christmas 1996, we worked to turn the gym—the one locals once referred to as "Auschwitz"—into a place of life, not death. Instead of planting bullets in people's foreheads, our workers wore smiles on their faces as they handed out gifts to the children of Hadzici. And guess which building we chose as the central distribution point? You're right—the gym where Laris's mother had been killed.

Al Denson of Dallas, Texas, and members of the Praise Band held a concert in front of the wall of execution, the very wall where Laris kicked his soccer ball day after day, and where so many of Hadzici's citizens had been slaughtered. Instead of screams and cries of agony emanating from that wall, beautiful music and generous gifts poured out of that place. As the band belted out the well-known praise hymn "Blessed be the Name of the Lord," children squealed with delight as they opened up their shoe boxes packed with love.

I sat above the crowd on a bleacher with my friend Mark DeMoss and absorbed the incredible sight and felt the satisfaction that comes from seeing the power of light overcome the darkness. Instead of families being torn apart by death, this day they were being brought together by love. Little kids perched on their father's shoulders. Mothers held tiny infants close to them.

And they were smiling, laughing, giggling. On every face, in every corner, "Auschwitz" had been turned into a place of celebration. What were we celebrating? Christmas, the birth of Jesus Christ. Christ's love was being presented to a Muslim village.

To the villagers of Hadzici, we were Christians who had cared enough to come to them in their darkest hours of despair and share with their children some treasured gifts. I think that many of them understood a deeper reality. Those who had witnessed the cruelty of hatred and ethnic cleansing firsthand were able to witness the contrasting love of Christ. We didn't speak their language and they didn't speak ours—but everybody understands love. We don't need a translator to understand a little boy's mile-wide smile. We don't need an interpreter to explain why a Bosnian girl is jumping up and down as she pulls a new doll out of the box.

"You Christians, you're the only ones who help us."

Is that true of your church? Is that true in your neighborhood? Is that true of you? You won't be able to meet everyone's needs, but are you willing to reach out in Christ's love and meet at least one?

The apostle John said, *"Love one another; as I have loved you. . . . By this all will know that you are My disciples, if you have love for one another"* (John 13:34–35).

M U D S L I D E

ATE ONE AFTERNOON my secretary received a disturbing call from a reporter. I was out of town, but he asked that she get a message to me as soon as possible.

"Tell Franklin we're breaking a story on tonight's news that will cost Jim Bakker his ministry. I would like to get a statement from him for the evening broadcast, which goes on the air soon."

My secretary called me right away.

But how could I comment on something that I knew nothing about? How could I know then that the mudslide was about to begin? Ever since Watergate, when *The Washington Post* investigated Richard Nixon, our society has accepted investigative reporting as a way of life.

For the next several months, the PTL saga provided endless fodder for the tabloid news media as accusations concerning the management of the ministry surfaced. The tabloids stereotyped and ridiculed Christians and mocked the gospel. Donations to many Christian organizations fell. Unfortunately, when scandals arise in the church, the devil will do his best to bring shame upon the name of Christ; sometimes the devil will even use Christians to do his clever work.

It saddened me to see the Christian media jump on the bandwagon with the secular media. I question the motives of Christians who sling mud by reporting scandals within the body of Christ. They defend it, saying it's their obligation. The Scripture carefully warns: *"If you keep on biting and devouring each other, watch out or you will be destroyed by each other"* (Gal. 5:15 NIV). There are very clear guidelines for discipline within the context of a church, but I see nowhere in the Scripture where we are publicly to announce a fallen brother or sister's sins before nonbelievers and the rest of the world. In fact, Ephesians 5:12 says, *"For it is shameful even to mention what the disobedient do in secret"* (NIV).

This might sound surprising, but when a moral failure occurs, God can still use these situations for His glory; however, this will not occur simply by exposing the scandal and announcing it to the world. Perhaps here, more than anywhere else, is where we desperately need to stay in sync with God. Jesus Christ is glorified when we stand by our brothers and sisters in Christ, loving them, rebuking them if need be, correcting them, and maybe even getting in their faces, but doing it in love. The book of Proverbs outlines six things (6:16) that the Lord hates—but the seventh is detestable to Him: *"A man who stirs up dissension among brothers"* (6:19 NIV).

We live in an age of scandals. If we want to walk in sync with God, we must learn the proper way to respond to failures. Maybe *you* are one of those who has fallen. If so, I've got good news for you: You can get back in sync with God and live beyond the limits by learning a few important things.

FORTY-FIVE YEARS!

Following the Bakker trial, I heard on the news that Jim had received his prison sentence: forty-five years! I felt sick to my stomach. Frequently murderers, rapists, and child molesters get a much less sentence for their crimes. It just didn't make sense. Sure, Jim had done some things wrong. He admits this himself in his own story *I Was Wrong*. But forty-five years in prison!

Immediately I thought to myself, *I was his friend in the good times. I'm going to stick by him in the bad times.* I couldn't change the length of Jim's sentence, but I thought perhaps I might be able to lessen the agony of it. I prayed and asked the Lord to show me what I could do to reach out to him.

When I learned that Jim had been sent to a prison in Rochester, Minnesota, I wrote him, offering to come and hold a service for the inmates.

Jim responded carefully that he was not in a position to authorize or even suggest anything. He was simply an inmate. But he recommended I talk to the prison chaplain's office. I called soon after and extended my offer to come and bring a group of musicians.

"We'll think about it," was the icy reply.

I wasn't asking to take Jim out of jail—I just wanted to visit him and hold a service to encourage the inmates. But the chaplain acted like he was doing me a big favor by "thinking about it." He also told me that if I wanted to see Jim personally, I would have to send a written request at least thirty days in advance.

I thought, *I can get to Angola in two days, and it's gonna take me thirty to work out a brief visit with Jim?*

I sent the requested letter. Permission to hold the service was finally granted under very strict rules and a date was set, but the chaplain told me, "I can't guarantee you a visit with Jim Bakker. This is our policy and procedure. Neither can you mention his name publicly while in the facility or ask for any kind of response during your service."

Now, I know it sounds funny for chaplains to tell an evangelist not to extend an altar call, but that's exactly what they said. For whatever reason, these people were cold.

I called Dennis Agajanian and his brother, Danny, to ask if they wanted to go with me to Rochester. Dennis and Danny are no strangers to men behind bars. They've played in hundreds of prisons, and as I expected, both were eager to accompany me.

Behind Bars

We arrived at the prison on a bleak January day. It took about an hour to sign in. The guard scanned our identification and checked it against a master log. We were given lengthy forms to fill out and instructed to empty our pockets. The warden then guided us through metal detectors, followed by a series of small, locked chambers.

When we stepped through the first electric gate, it jarred shut behind us, but we faced another one immediately ahead. For a brief moment, we were locked inside the small holding cell. Once the bars behind us slammed firmly into place, the door in front began to jerk and slide open. As soon as we stepped through, the gate begin to glide shut with a clink of the metal. We got the clear impression that nobody was going anywhere fast.

The air inside the prison was very stale—obviously a fresh breeze blowing through open windows was a thing of the past for the prison residents. And the most pervasive putrid yellow paint covered the walls. It reminded me of vanilla ice cream that has been left in the freezer too long. To be in this environment and escape the effects of depression would be quite a feat.

Everywhere we looked, cameras were monitoring our every move. Guards peered through bulletproof panes, glaring at us as if we were criminals. We kept reminding ourselves that we were just visiting and would be able to leave in a few hours. I gained new sympathy for Jim, imagining what it must have felt like to be sentenced to this environment for a dreadful forty-five years.

We were finally led into the prison yard and across to an adjacent building, where we followed the guard into a large room that had been set up for the service. Dennis and Danny and one of my staff members, Rick Auten, began setting up the equipment and running through the sound checks. Ironically, before Rick had joined my staff, he had been a cameraman for Jim Bakker at PTL.

I finally spotted the chaplain and asked about Jim. The chaplain shifted uneasily on his feet. "Well, he may or may not be here."

"Why not?"

"To tell you the truth, we're not even sure he knows you're coming."

I was angry, of course, but I didn't dare show it. All I could do was pray that God would make a way for Jim to attend the meeting.

A group of prisoners had formed in the back rows, their arms folded across their chests, listening to the instruments being tuned. Through the back door inmates started pouring in. But one man, in spite of his uniformity with black, steel-tipped shoes and gray prison clothes, stood out. I squinted to sharpen my view—sure enough, it was my friend, Jim Bakker. I was up on my feet and to the back wall before he could spot me.

Rick Auten was right behind me. We grabbed hold of Jim's hands and he clasped ours, as the prisoners watched. That handshake said volumes. Jim was visibly moved.

I could tell Jim felt renewed when he could say to the other inmates, "Hey, this guy [Rick] used to work for me." It was his way of affirming, *My life used to be worth something. My friends have come to visit me.* For a whiff of a moment, a little dignity had come back into Jim's life. Loyalty is a rare thing in our society. If a former employer or friend runs into trouble, most often we scatter like buckshot.

Rick and Jim spent a few minutes talking about PTL, and Jim was briefly transported outside the prison walls, if only in his memories. Seeing Rick reminded him that he hadn't always lived in such a drab, dreary place. His reminiscing wasn't a fabrication; it was a real, though distant, memory.

Jim and I talked for a few minutes. He maintained that (in his words) he was wrongfully imprisoned "like the apostle Paul." I listened sympathetically as he justified his actions to me, but I couldn't offer my total agreement—caring for the fallen doesn't always mean agreeing with them. The apostle Paul was not a convicted felon. Jim was. In my eyes, there is a big difference.

But the basis of what Jim was saying made sense to me. I don't believe he ever intended to defraud anybody. He simply allowed himself to get out of sync with God's will. Maybe he thought that God would somehow overlook his sins and failures because he was doing so much for God.

This is an important point. Sometimes there's nothing more than a fine line between being in the will of God and being out of the will of God, but that very fine line makes a huge difference. A little bit out of sync is still out of sync, which knocks us completely off balance. There's no part-time fellowship with God.

In 2 Chronicles 15:2 Asa, king of Judah, is told, *"The LORD is with you while you are with Him. If you seek Him, He will be found by you; but if you forsake Him, He will forsake you."* Judah and Israel left God; they got out of sync, but over time, it led them to get way off the mark. The result? *"For a long time Israel has been without the true God, without a teaching priest, and without law"* (2 Chron. 15:3).

If I had flown from Boone, North Carolina, to Rochester with my compass just a few degrees off, even though I was flying in the right direction (due north), by the time I arrived I might be in the state of Minnesota, but I would be entirely off course and miles from Rochester. Many times we think we are going the right direction in life and don't realize that the little decisions we make will determine whether we stay on course. We can miss our target by just a few degrees. If you get out of step with God, watch out. You're in a dangerous position.

STILL SERVING GOD

As Jim and I continued to visit, a guard signaled that we could begin the program. The rigid regulations imposed didn't overshadow the Agajanians's thunder. Dennis and Danny started with, of all songs, "Folsom Prison Blues." It was electric—the inmates went wild. Many of the prisoners sang along as the guys played old bluegrass tunes, finally finishing with some grand old hymns.

After the concert was over I gave a short, evangelistic message. I spoke about Manasseh, the wickedest man in the Bible, a man who had led Israel into more sin than any other man. His father, Hezekiah, had been a good man, but when Manasseh became king at age twelve, he began shaking his fist in God's face from that point on. In fact, he was determined to undo everything good that his father had done. He led Israel into immorality. He instituted child sacrifice and even sacrificed his own child in the fire to Moloch. He built high places to worship other gods, in direct contradiction to God's holy command, "*You shall have no other gods before Me*" (Ex. 20:3).

Manasseh led Israel to shed so much innocent blood that the Bible says, "*He had filled Jerusalem from one end to another*" (2 Kings 21:16). In fact, Manasseh led Israel into more error than had the heathen kings whom God had cast out of the land to make way for Israel!

God eventually judges sin, and He brought judgment on Manasseh. He used the Babylonians to conquer Israel, destroy Jerusalem, and carry Manasseh off to prison. Humbled by his fall, Manasseh dared to call upon God for forgiveness. God heard his prayer from within those prison walls, forgave him, and restored him. Manasseh went back to Israel, tore down the high places, and called all Israel to worship the King of kings and the Lord of lords.

"No matter what you've done," I told the prisoners, "God will forgive you if you're willing to call upon His name. He will hear you even from inside these prison walls, just like He heard Manasseh."

I was determined to honor my word not to give an altar call, but I made sure every inmate knew when he returned to his cell exactly how he could find salvation in Christ.

Following the meeting, the prisoners came forward to shake my hand. Some wanted autographs and even asked for photos. These men were not accustomed to having visitors, and they all seemed sincerely grateful. Jim was standing behind my right shoulder and whispered each man's name as he filed by. In those moments I learned something special about Jim.

He knew every name, what each one was in prison for, and—even more important—where each one was spiritually.

A stocky, athletic, dark-complexioned man walked up and Jim said, "That's Raul. He's a Colombian, in for drugs, but he just gave his heart to Christ three weeks ago and we're studying the Bible together."

A white man walked up. "That's John," Jim coached. "He's from a middle-class background and is in for tax evasion. He's not a believer yet, but he's close, and we're all praying for him."

It touched my heart to see Jim serving God, even behind bars. The secular world doesn't realize the power of repentance and forgiveness, mercy and restoration, but I had a feeling that the Lord was beginning to make a change in Jim's life.

A DIFFERENT MAN

My second visit with Jim occurred about a year and a half later. Jim had been moved to a new prison facility in Jesup, Georgia, and the chaplains there were very different from those in Rochester. They weren't just government bureaucrats or employees putting in their time. They had a genuine sense of their spiritual responsibility.

When I asked them about visiting the prison, they said, "Mr. Graham, we'd love to have you any time, and we'd be glad for you to bring anyone you can. Our inmates would be thrilled."

"Could I have some private time with Jim Bakker?" I asked.

"Sure," came the enthusiastic response. "We can arrange that."

When I arrived, I met Jim in a common visitation area with vending machines lined up against the walls. A number of inmates were there with their families, and the spirit in the room seemed lighthearted. As I talked with several of them, I was amazed at how many had become believers. Their concern for each other was genuine, and a spirit of brotherly love pervaded the room. I've seen more tension and backbiting at church picnics and potlucks than I saw there!

I realized as Jim and I talked that he was a different man. He was no longer defending himself. Instead, he told me, "Franklin, I was wrong. God is the One who put me in this prison, and God will release me in His time."

I couldn't believe it. Was this the same Jim Bakker I had visited in Rochester just one year before, defending his actions? Jim was humble. He repeated over and over, "I was wrong." I could see God's hand in his life, and I thought, *God isn't through with Jim Bakker. Jim's best years are still ahead.*

I was reminded of John 15:1–2: *"I am the true vine, and My Father is the vinedresser. Every branch in Me that does not bear fruit He takes away; and every branch that bears fruit He prunes, that it may bear more fruit."*

Jim, like all of us, needed to have a few branches cut off from time to time. Yet the Lord saw there was something good that could bear fruit. This is true of every believer who wants to be effective in Christ and walk in sync with Him. God will prune us so that we will remain in Him and grow stronger.

Jesus' teaching reveals the heart of God, and He wants to reach out to the hurting through His children.

> *For I was hungry and you gave me something to eat, I was*
> *thirsty and you gave me something to drink, I was a stranger*
> *and you invited me in, I needed clothes and you clothed me,*
> *I was sick and you looked after me, I was in prison and you*

came to visit me. . . . I tell you the truth, whatever you did for one of the least of these brothers of mine, you did for me. (Matt. 25:35–36, 40 NIV)

HELPING THE HURTING

J IM'S FORTY-FIVE-YEAR SENTENCE was reduced to eight years, and he was ultimately released to a halfway house in Asheville, North Carolina, after serving five years because of "good behavior." The Sunday after Jim left the Federal Correctional Institution in Jesup, Georgia, I was scheduled to preach at my parent's home church in Montreat, just outside of Asheville. I contacted Jim's attorney and asked him to extend an invitation for Jim to attend the service. The attorney was skeptical that Jim would be comfortable accepting, but I assured him that Jim would be well received. *I'll seat him right next to Mama,* I thought. *Nobody will dare say a word about him being there if he's sitting with her.*

Dr. Calvin Thielman, my parents' pastor (as well as my boyhood pastor), is a straight-shootin' (I know, because he shot himself in the leg when I was a boy!), slow-talkin' Texan. I called Calvin to ask if he would foresee a problem with Jim coming.

"No problem at all," he said. "He's welcome."

"Calvin, do you think you'll get any flak from the elders?"

"No way. And even if I do, so what? Right is right, and inviting Jim to church is the right thing to do."

That's what I've always loved about Calvin. He never was much for political correctness.

I'm grateful that I was raised in a home where the example of reaching out to the downcast was evident. I remember watching my mother and father offering a helping hand to those who had made mistakes and were truly repentant.

As a little boy, when Daddy was gone on his crusades, I watched my mother seek out the lonely, far-from-home college student who was in need of an adopted family for an afternoon. Instead of feeling sorry for herself that she had been left alone herself, she sought to care for others. My mother was the type of woman who always brought the stray cat home. If she found a lost puppy, she'd scoop that dirty animal into her arms, feed it, and care for it until its owner could be found.

My father has been known to do the same. He managed to get a few chuckles during a 1997 San Antonio crusade by pleading for somebody to feed a hungry cat that he had come across on a local college campus. The poor thing was so thin that Daddy felt sorry for it. "If you know who owns that cat," he told the laughing crowd, "tell them it's hungry and needs to eat."

If we help lost animals, shouldn't we reach out to people living in anguishing circumstances?

My parents have a heart for Christians experiencing difficulties, like Jim Bakker, so much so that they built The Cove. Daddy asked me years ago to help him with the project. The overall purpose of The Cove is to train Christians in God's Word, but it was built with a smaller side-mission in mind.

Located just outside Asheville, North Carolina, The Cove is built on 1,500 beautiful mountain acres. Some of the world's finest Bible teachers come to teach the Scriptures to lay people. Yet hidden away on this property are some remote cabins that my parents offer to well-known individuals who need privacy. It is a place for them to pray and seek God's face in difficult times, to study God's Word, and to begin slowly to put their lives back together.

Even more important than following my parents' example in reaching out to others is to follow God's commandment.

HELPING A FRIEND

Jim had only been out of prison for one day when his lawyer brought him to Montreat Presbyterian Church. I had an assistant, Bryan Willis, bring Jim to Calvin's office in the back of the church. I felt for Jim. He was nervous and fidgety, like he didn't belong. His eyes darted around the room as if he couldn't focus on any one thing. I finally asked him if something was wrong.

"Franklin," he explained, "after years of being cooped up behind bars, it's like seeing the outside world for the first time. I am amazed by the beauty of it all."

Calvin put his arms around Jim, hugged him, and welcomed him. We had a chance for a private visit before church and prayed together. Calvin asked Jim if there was any one thing that stuck out in his mind about his prison experience.

Jim broke down and cried. Through his sobs he said, "Franklin and others came to visit me in prison. You'll never know what it means when someone comes to visit you in such a horrible place."

I felt rebuked because I hadn't done more. The Bible tells us to visit those in prison. The Bible doesn't say visit only the nonguilty. It says, visit those in prison, period. If we want to touch the heart of God, and walk in step with Him, we have to take Him at His Word. And where does He walk? Through the prison wards and in the ditches and gutters of this world, not just in ivory palaces. Remember, God's Son was born in a stable.

Jim was a broken man—and completely repentant. I determined on the spot that I would do everything possible to help him. As we talked about the logistical requirements of his early release, I said, "Jim, let us help you with a place to live. We can find a car for you to use." Jim pulled me aside and said, "Franklin, you don't need me, and I'm afraid my old baggage could hurt you. If people find out you're doing this for me, it might tarnish your reputation—I'm a convicted felon."

I looked Jim straight in the eyes and said, "Jim, you're my friend. You were my friend before, and you're my friend now. Besides," I added, smiling, "if no one likes it, that's their problem."

The way I saw it, the ministry arms of Samaritan's Purse had been strengthened by Jim in years past; he had contributed so much to our work and others', the least we could do was to help him once he got out of prison.

As Jim began to regain composure, I said, "Bryan will escort you to the seat next to my mother. She's looking forward to being with you and has invited you and your son, Jamie, for dinner up at the house after the service. We'll talk then."

Jim thanked me and slipped in the back of the church, for the most part unnoticed. In my opening remarks that morning, I looked into the faces of the congregation and said, "Most of you have read in the papers that Jim Bakker has been released to a halfway house here in the Asheville area." I shared my recollection of what Jim had done for Samaritan's Purse years ago, and what Jim had done for the missionaries at Tenwek hospital in Africa by raising hundreds of thousands of dollars to build one of the most modern mission hospitals in all of Africa.

"The same Jim Bakker who helped build that hospital is visiting with us today." It gave me great satisfaction to introduce Jim as I remembered that day in the Rochester prison when the warden forbade me to mention Jim's name. I pointed toward the back of the sanctuary. "He's sitting with Mama. Jim, I'd like to have you stand."

As Jim hesitantly stood, this conservative southern Presbyterian church broke out into a sustained applause, welcoming Jim. Jim nodded, and with tears in his eyes, quickly sat down. Mama reached out and patted him on the hand, reassuring him of our love and support.

RESTORATION AT LITTLE PINEY COVE

Following the service Mama and I took Jim and Jamie to Little Piney Cove, a crooked mile or so from the church. We sat down in Mama's kitchen to enjoy a typical North Carolina Sunday meal — fried chicken, pork and beans, hush puppies (deep fried corn meal, for those who ain't from the South), potato salad, coleslaw, and buttermilk biscuits. It was fun watching Jim feast on the southern cookin'. He didn't know what to pick up first. He started laughing. "Mrs. Graham," he said, "in prison we didn't get *any* choices. We ate what was put in front of us. I look at this feast and want it all!"

Mama grinned and said, "Well, you can just have it all."

We all did a pretty good job devouring everything in sight. We especially enjoyed the fellowship around the table. As Mama was serving dessert, she asked Jim for his address. He reached into his pocket and pulled out a creased paper envelope in which he kept his addresses.

"What's that?" Mama asked.

"My wallet," Jim answered with a laugh. "You know, Mrs. Graham, prisoners are not allowed to have billfolds."

"Just a minute," Mama said. She left the table and walked back to the bedroom. When she returned moments later, she handed one of Daddy's wallets to Jim. He was visibly shaken. A fallen minister, convicted of financial wrongdoing, was being handed Billy Graham's billfold! It was a touching moment. (To this day, he still carries that wallet. I saw him pull it out during a recent interview with Larry King.)

As the afternoon slipped away, I could tell that Jim had begun to relax. Perhaps sharing a meal around the table gave him a sense of love and acceptance in Mama's homey little cove nestled in the hills far from the cell Jim never grew accustomed to. I feel certain that it helped Jim face public ridicule in the outside world with a little more confidence.

A JUST MAN IS QUIET

Have you ever received a parcel in the mail that's stamped FRAGILE: HANDLE WITH CARE? And when you open it, you can tell the postman did just that. But there are other times we receive packages and find the contents shattered. It generally means it has been mishandled in transit. Most likely you'll file an immediate claim for damages from the carrier who was irresponsible with your precious cargo. If we handle our valuables with tender, loving care, shouldn't we do the same with people? After all, people can crumble too.

In Matthew 1, we read about a man who did just that when he discovered the alleged sin of his pledged bride. The Bible tells us that Joseph, *"being a just man, and not wanting to make her* [Mary] *a public example, was minded to put her away secretly"* (v. 19). Now, we know that Mary didn't sin in the conception of our Lord, but Joseph knew that he wasn't the father of Mary's unborn child. In his mind, obviously, something was very wrong.

In a fit of rage and righteous indignation, Joseph could have had Mary stoned. He could have brought her out to the town square for public humiliation. He could have said, "Look how I have been wronged, how I have been deceived, how I have been violated." He could have taken Mary to the temple, brought his charges before the elders, had his engagement revoked, and then handed her over. If Joseph had done that, he would have fallen out of step with God's plan. He wouldn't have been blessed to serve as the earthly father of our Lord and Savior, Jesus Christ.

But Joseph was a just man. *I'll deal with it secretly,* he thought.

He knew God's heart, and God's way is always opposite of the way of the world. Joseph was a righteous man and did not want to expose her to public disgrace. As he was contemplating this, an angel of the Lord appeared to him in a dream and said, *"Joseph . . . do not be afraid to take Mary home as your wife. . . .'* When Joseph woke up, he did what the angel of the Lord had commanded him" (vv. 20, 24 NIV).

I have often wondered how the present-day Christian magazines would have covered an apparent scandalous story back then.

Man's way is to expose, to sell a lot of magazines, to boost circulation. Who cares that success comes at someone else's expense? Think about the bottom line. This is a business, you know. We need to get our subscriptions up. Then comes the righteous justification: It's our duty to the Lord and our mandate to the people. We have an obligation to the church.

It is a desperate attempt to gain more subscribers under the guise of a biblical mandate that doesn't exist. But instead of calling it what it really is, they hide their intentions by finding new ways to package an age-old sin: gossip.

James tells us to hold our tongue: *"But no man can tame the tongue. It is a restless evil, full of deadly poison. With the tongue we praise our Lord and Father, and with it we curse men, who have been made in God's likeness. Out of the same mouth come praise and cursing. My brothers, this should not be. Can both fresh water and salt water flow from the same spring?"* (James 3:8–11 NIV).

If we want to keep in sync with God, maybe we should consider responding to scandal by practicing the same method Shem and Japheth, two of Noah's sons, used.

STRIKING OUT

After the flood, Noah celebrated one harvest a little too much and got drunk. He went back to his tent, and as he was getting into bed, he must have passed out. He lay naked in his tent when his son Ham walked in on him. Ham should have covered his father and kept his mouth shut. Instead he felt he had some moral duty to announce his father's drunkenness to his brothers and thereby expose his father's failure and weakness.

God tells us to honor our mother and father, but Ham dishonored Noah.

Strike one.

Ham could have covered his father himself, but he didn't.

Strike two.

Instead, Ham went outside and told his brothers about their drunken dad.

Strike three.

Was there glee in Ham's voice when he told of his father's shame? We don't know. We do know, however, that his brothers responded God's way. Shem and Japheth immediately took a garment, laid it on both their shoulders, and, walking backward, covered the nakedness of their father. Their faces were turned away, and they did not see their father's shame (Gen. 9:23).

Shem and Japheth didn't want to see their father in his sin. There was no illicit pleasure in gossiping about what they had heard. All they wanted to do was quietly administer a solution. Their intentions were pure and in sync with God's heart.

Ham's way was the world's way: Tell it all, expose it! And for that, not only was he cursed, but his son was cursed as well. The Bible says that God will *"repay the iniquity of the fathers into the bosom of their children after them"* (Jer. 32:18).

When someone's sin is uncovered, what are we to do? Call the Associated Press? Sell the story to the *National Enquirer?* Write it up in the church bulletin? Send a fax to a Christian magazine?

None of that. We are called to love and forgive the fallen. First Corinthians 13:5 says: Love *"keeps no record of wrongs"* (NIV). So, then, what's the motive of exposing? It's usually based in self-righteousness, greed, and the individual's own sense of guilt. We report about other scandals because it takes the attention off our own personal failures. God doesn't excuse our sins because someone else has sinned in a more public way. We're still responsible for what we do.

This sin of gossiping has been around the church for a long time. Back in the sixth century, a monk named John Climacus chastised those he called "accountants of other people's faults." John wrote, "I have rebuked people who were engaged in slander, and, in self-defense, these evildoers claimed to be acting out of love and concern for the victim of their slander. My answer to that was to say: 'Then stop that kind of love, or else you will be making a liar out of him who declared, "I drove away the man who secretly slandered his neighbor" [Ps. 101:5].'"

By saying this, however, I don't mean to imply that we should be soft on sin. The Bible clearly states that sin should be confronted privately and in love, leading those who have stumbled along the way into repentance and restoration.

LEAVING IT IN GOD'S HANDS

I believe in preaching without compromise against sin. As we watch our Judeo-Christian values slip away in the present age of "anything goes," I have discovered that people do not know what sin is; because of this their lifestyle is an offense to God. Hearts are so hardened to sin that people truly don't recognize it any more.

I was holding crusade meetings in Australia in 1996 and met with a group of pastors in Sydney one morning for breakfast. Several informed me that their countrymen truly did not know how to define sin. Many churchgoers thought that as long as they attended church, they were bound for heaven.

That bit of table talk prompted me to begin incorporating the Ten Commandments in their entirety in each sermon. "Lying is a sin," I'll carefully point out from the pulpit. "Stealing is a sin— whether you steal from your neighbor, the government, or a big business, it's still a sin. It's wrong. Having sex outside the bonds of marriage between a man and a woman is a sin. Letting anything become a god in your life is a sin—whether that god is athletics, your vocation, your prominence and reputation, or your financial security, it doesn't matter. If it comes before God, it's idolatry. It's a sin. Using God's name without respect is wrong; it's not 'funny' to God. Dishonoring your parents is wrong. All of these things are sinfully wicked in the eyes of God."

God hates sin, but the good news is that He loves the sinner. Sin needs to be confessed and renounced. There may come a time when, as the last resort in a long process, a church needs to finally and publicly address an unrepentant member; but nowhere in the Bible is the church urged to publicize these proceedings for the entire world to read so they can laugh. The individual church body needs to handle discipline within the confines of its own and keep it there.

Like Noah's faithful sons, we need to learn how to take care of scandals within the household of faith.

My mother drilled an important lesson into my head at an early age: *"If you can't say anything nice, don't say anything at all."* When I tend to forget this, she has some pretty creative ways of reminding me. I thank God for a wise mother.

There will always be sin in the church because it is made up of imperfect people—sinners saved by God's grace. Something else that will always be around are leaders who fail. Every generation has had to weather at least one scandal. Because I've grown up as the son of Billy Graham, I've come to know many well-known leaders. Every one of them will admit to certain personal shortcomings.

On the other hand, God can and does use sinful people. I can certainly identify with the apostle Paul, who wrote in 1 Timothy 1:15: *"Christ Jesus came into the world to save sinners—of whom I am the worst"* (NIV). I am a sinner who deserves God's judgment, but God forgave me. There isn't a single Christian who doesn't fall short of Christ's example and who doesn't need to repent on a daily basis.

A. B. Simpson said, "I would rather play with forked lightning, or take in my hand living wires with their fiery current, than speak a reckless word against any servant of Christ, or idly repeat the slanderous darts which thousands of Christians are hurling on others, to the hurt of their own souls and bodies." God will sort everything out when we get to heaven, so we can put away our knives.

Some of us, like Mary, will be falsely accused. Others, like Noah and David, will really blow it and deserve censure. But the Bible doesn't call us to act as self-appointed judges, prosecutors, or jury. Those are roles God reserves for Himself, and it's a role that is best left to Him. The Scripture carefully instructs us:

> Brothers, if someone is caught in a sin, you who are spiritual should restore him gently. But watch yourself, or you also may be tempted. Carry each other's burdens, and in this way you will fulfill the law of Christ. (Gal. 6:1–2 NIV)

I urge you, when you find someone who has fallen, take the high road. Refuse to gossip. Instead, contain it. Confront him privately in love and lead him into repentance so that he can experience God's forgiveness. Help that person get back in fellowship with God. This is how we keep in sync with Him.

God says in His Word, "*Brethren, if anyone among you wanders from the truth, and someone turns him back, let him know that he who turns a sinner from the error of his way will save a soul from death and cover a multitude of sins*" (James 5:19–20).

I have seen Jim Bakker on many occasions since that Sunday lunch at my mother's log home in Little Piney Cove. I have observed him at a distance while being interviewed by some of the most seasoned, cynical reporters in the world today.

Jim has answered tough questions directly and honestly. He has taken the blame for his mistakes and has owned up to the fact that he was wrong. It is a testimony to what God can do in a life when confession of sin is made in true repentance. The lesson for all of us is, when we sin don't excuse it. Do as Jim has humbly done: Accept responsibility and ask God's forgiveness and begin anew. I thank God for Jim's example and am glad to be called his friend.

A S PRESIDENT OF SAMARITAN'S PURSE, my responsibilities and ministry frequently take me away from home. God blessed me with a wonderful wife, who is also a terrific mother to our four children. Anyone who knows Jane Austin knows that she is a gutsy woman. And it's a good thing. We live on a little farm way out in the hill country where strangers and stray critters often appear. When I leave home—sometimes for days—it's a comfort to know that my children and home are in capable hands.

When our kids were young, some neighbor boys who live down the dirt road came running up to our house. Breathlessly, they bounded up the wooden steps and banged their fists on the door. "Miss Jane, Miss Jane, there's a snake down thar in the creek!"

Jane Austin started laughing as she went to the shelf and got the Smith & Wesson 357 Magnum. She picked up our youngest at the time—Edward, who was eighteen months old—and headed down the hill toward the creek, calling our other two boys, Will and Roy, to follow.

The neighbor boys were right on her heels, panting all the way, with excitement in their voices and a tinge of fear in their eyes. When she approached the creek's bank, it didn't take her long to spot the slithering serpent down in the cool mountain water. As she balanced Edward on her hip, she steadied the gun and aimed it toward the rippling water. Looking around to make sure all the little ones were safely behind her, she cocked the trigger and plastered a bullet into the snake's head.

"You hit him, Miss Jane, you got him!" the younger boy yelled, jumping up and down, clapping his hands, and shouting. "Shoot him again, shoot him again."

"Nah, she don't need to," the older boy said with a slow drawl. "She done blowed his head off."

Now when folks ask how my wife handles me being gone so much, I often grin and tell them that little story as I watch their eyes grow wide with disbelief. If it weren't for Jane Austin's love of the outdoors and country livin', it would have been difficult for my children to grow up like I did. She's a lady who can hold her own.

But she is also very sensitive. Like most mothers, she would give her life to protect our kids as well as other children who live around us. I have seen how God has used her to comfort young mothers when their children were sick or troubled. She is always ready to lend a listening ear and a helping hand to those who are hurting and in need. These are the qualities that attracted me to Jane Austin when we were young. She reminds me of my mother, who can hang tough in the hard times, and be tenderhearted toward others experiencing difficulties in their own lives.

I was fortunate to have Jane Austin with me in South Africa when I was holding crusade meetings there. While in Johannesburg, we visited a children's cancer ward in the largest hospital in the world located in the Lanasia district. She helped with our distribution of gifts to the children, giving each of them a shoe box collected through our Operation Christmas Child project.

We were joined by Christian recording artists Michael W. Smith (we call him Smitty) and Dennis Agajanian. As we walked through the hallways lined with wards, the little ones began to peer out from behind doors and around bed railings. Dennis started playing his guitar, and the children began to fill the hallway. They huddled together watching Dennis intently as his fingers flew across the strings. They began to clap their hands to the music, and Smitty started singing "Jesus Loves Me." Jane Austin and I stood back against the wall and looked at the little children enjoying a moment of pleasure. Some had lost their hair, others their limbs. Our hearts grew heavy, knowing that many of these kids would face death soon.

While the guys continued to sing, Jane Austin slipped away. I began to look around and finally spotted her coming down the hall holding a little baby, about fourteen months old. She had gone into the wards to play with the little ones who were too sick to come out into the hall to join in the excitement.

When she walked into the last ward, she found a little girl sitting up in a crib clapping her hands to the faint rhythm of Dennis's guitar. The child had patches over her eyes and a bandage around her head. Cancer had blinded her. Jane Austin picked her up and rocked her for a while and then carried her down the hall to where the other children were assembled.

The child began to smile as she grew closer to the sound of the music. Jane Austin walked right up to Dennis and laid the child's hand on his instrument. The little girl's face lit up like a glistening star as she felt the vibration of the guitar. It was hard to hold back the tears.

The thing that moved me moments later was to watch my ten-year-old daughter, Cissie, in another ward. She had found her own infant patient to hold, comfort, and love. It occurred to me how much she reminded me of her mama, and I thanked God for the example of the gentle touch of a mother's love that was spread through the ward that day.

God has enabled us to reach out to the lost and hurting of this world through the work of Samaritan's Purse. Because of Jane Austin's love for others, she has been a source of strength to me in my ministry and a tremendous example for my children in life. I think of the Proverbs 31: "*Her husband has full confidence in her and lacks nothing of value. She brings him good, not harm. . . . She opens her arms to the poor and extends her hands to the needy. . . . Her children arise and call her blessed; her husband also, and he praises her*" (vv. 11–12, 20, 28 NIV).

To be able to live beyond human limits, we must surround ourselves with wise and honest counsel. Most would agree that it is important to marry a wise mate; someone who has your best interests at heart. It is also important to include in your circle of friends those who are wise and seek God in their lives. Proverbs 13:20 says: "*He who walks with the wise grows wise*" (NIV).

I grew up living and working around strong, capable women who, in wisdom, walk with God. In my early years, my life was impacted by my mother and grandmothers. Later, in Jordan, I encountered Aileen Coleman and Dr. Eleanor Soltau who had a profound impact on me. A few years later, I married Jane Austin. I have the freedom to do the work God has called me to because I have a wife who supports me and keeps the home fires burning.

I was only twenty-eight years old when I was called to the leadership of Samaritan's Purse. Though I graduated from the university with a business degree, I really didn't have any experience in running an office, communicating to donors, keeping the books, or scheduling doctors to serve in mission hospitals. Believe me, I had my hands full.

Fortunately, God has brought a number of tremendously talented people to Samaritan's Purse. Much of the work is run and managed by extremely capable women. Not only do they all share a love for the ministry, but more important, they have an unshakable faith in our Lord Jesus Christ. Everything they do reflects their walk with Him. They set a standard for the entire organization to follow.

When a national men's ministry asked to meet with our management team, I surprised them by stating that many of our top managers are women. I respect women and thank God for their insight.

If you're a woman who wants to get in sync with God, it's important for you to understand the mighty things God has done through women in the past. Scripture is full of stories that extol the special virtues of women who know how to touch the heart of God, who walk with Him, and who are eager to be used by Him and live a life that is beyond the culture of stereotypes.

One of those women is named Jael.

A WOMAN'S COURAGE

Jael was a simple Bedouin woman who lived near the terebinth tree at a place called Zaanaim. Virtually every woman who lived in her day—the age of the Israelite judges, between Moses and David—died in complete anonymity. There are no graves to mark their bodies; no monuments to tell of their exploits.

Part of this is because Jael happened to be born in a time and a place when women weren't valued for much beyond their ability to bear children and care for their husbands. They could be divorced on a whim and would thus be cast into a life of unavoidable destitution. Unfortunately, this attitude toward women still exists in many countries around the world. I have personally seen this in Africa, Asia, and the Middle East.

During times of war—and in the period of the judges—it was particularly perilous to be a woman. If an enemy defeated your husband, brothers, and father, there would be no one to protect you from the pillaging, victorious army. Women, gold, livestock, and anything else that could be carried off were considered fair game, a part of the spoils of war.

Imagine being forced to serve the man who you knew was responsible for killing your mother, your father, your husband, or your children. The blood of your kinsmen might still literally be on his hands as he carried you away with a wink and a grin. In such circumstances, being an attractive woman was a curse—remember how Abraham continued to lie about Sarah, his wife. He was afraid Pharaoh would kill him because Pharaoh found her so beautiful (Gen. 12:14).

In the Scripture, we read about God raising up different women who would break out of these constricting circumstances and, with God's power, distinguish themselves in remarkable ways. Jael was one of these women. Her imprint on history came as the result of a victorious Israelite army—which, ironically enough, was led by another woman, a judge named Deborah.

Jabin, king of Canaan, had ruled over the Israelites and enslaved them with an iron grip for twenty years. He oppressed the sons of Abraham, but they refused to rebel against him for fear of his formidable command of nine hundred "chariots of iron."

While the men quaked, a woman named Deborah listened to the Lord, and the Lord told her, *Attack.* Israel's most able commander at the time, a man named Barak, refused to go unless Deborah led the way. She agreed and led the men into battle against the mighty Canaanites.

Jabin's feared commander, Sisera, met the Israelites at the River Kishon. Barak's men charged down Mount Tabor and crashed into the Canaanite army.

So far, so good, Sisera thought. *This really shouldn't take that long. The Israelites don't have a single chariot among them.*

Yet Sisera watched in horror as his army fell apart under his command. In terror, Sisera fled on foot until he found himself gasping for air outside the tent of Heber. Jael invited him in, gave him some warm milk, and covered him with a blanket. Sisera then ordered Jael to lie for him if anyone should inquire as to his whereabouts.

As soon as Sisera went to sleep, however, Jael went to work. She went outside and pulled up a tent peg. She then rummaged around in the tent until she found a hammer. I'm sure her hands were sweating, but the enemy of Israel was sleeping before her, and she had a duty to perform.

Carefully, so as not to wake the commander, Jael placed the tent peg on his forehead and then lifted the hammer, driving the peg through the brain of Israel's feared enemy, killing him and thus freeing the people of God.

A God Who Honors Women

Growing up reading Bible stories like this one, which was taken from Judges 4, it's not surprising to me that God chooses to use women in so many powerful ways. Religion has often subdued women and kept them under foot, but true Christianity in Scripture frees them. Scripture is very honest with the fact that at His arrest, Jesus was abandoned by most of His disciples, while the women faithfully sought to prepare His body for burial.

In fact, Jesus first appeared to women after His resurrection. Think about it: The gospel in its entirety was first revealed to women. When they came to the open tomb, the angels admonished, *"Go quickly and tell His disciples that He is risen"* (Matt. 28:7). As they hurried to find the eleven, Jesus Himself appeared before them and said, *"Go and tell my brothers"* (Matt. 28:10 NIV). In a very real sense, you could call these women the first evangelists.

I wouldn't be the person I am today if my mother hadn't been the strong woman God made her to be. I've also been blessed with some gifted siblings, including my three sisters, Bunny, Anne, and Gigi. We're going to discover that while God uses many men, He also uses just as many women—women who have learned to trust God and offer themselves for His service.

Breakfast with the President

On January 1, 1997, I was hunting with my son Roy and our friend Sterling Carroll at his ranch in West Texas. I called Mama to wish her a Happy New Year. During the conversation, I told her that I had been invited to a breakfast at the White House with some ecumenical leaders the next week. President Clinton had invited a number of so-called religious leaders to gather so that he could outline his policies on welfare and immigration and talk about how the religious community could pick up some of the slack. I've never considered myself a religious leader, but I accepted the invitation. My mother told me that my sister (Anne Lotz) had also been invited. She suggested that we go together.

Anne is as outspoken as she is conservative. She is also probably one of the most dynamic speakers—male or female—that I know. When she speaks, she does so with authority and power. Though she has great tact, she won't use false flattery. I wondered if the President knew what he was getting himself into by inviting her.

I picked Anne up in Raleigh, and the two of us flew together to Washington. While we were having dinner that evening, a question came to mind: "Anne, if you were to be seated at the President's table tomorrow morning, what would you say to him?" Never did I dream that would really happen.

The next morning we mingled with the other guests, and then were directed into another room for the meeting. I took my assigned place and was shortly joined by Vice President Al Gore. I looked behind me, and lo and behold there was Anne seated at the President's table. *This could be interesting,* I thought.

The conversation at the Vice President's table was lighthearted—chitchat about the upcoming NFL playoffs, the Charlotte Panthers' chances, that kind of thing—but somehow I doubted the conversation at the table where Anne was seated was so trivial.

After we had finished eating, the media were invited in and lined up at the back of the room. The President stood and gave his speech on immigration and welfare reform. There was light applause when he finished, and then the media were escorted out. As soon as the press cleared the room, the President said, "Now I would like to hear from all of you."

It seemed every faith was represented in that room: Roman Catholics, Baptists, Eastern Orthodox Christians, Muslims, Jews, Pentecostals, you name it. Representatives stood one after the other and lauded the President's plans. "Mr. President," one leader said, "you're right. I accept your challenge for our congregations to adopt people on welfare." Another said, "Mr. President, I came from Eastern Europe, and if it wasn't for the open immigration policies of the United States, I wouldn't be here."

I thought to myself, *Why have we come? What kind of useful information is the President getting by having a cheering section where everybody just pats him on the back?*

I was disappointed that these religious leaders were not focusing on spiritual issues. *Not a single person is going to question the President's policies or offer a different opinion,* I thought.

I was sitting no more than five or six feet away from where the President stood behind the lectern. I wondered, *Am I the only one who thinks this way?*

I suppose I could have spoken up, but I felt out of place—these were articulate policy makers, the President's cabinet, high-ranking bishops in uniform, monks, and imams, many dressed in flowing robes that swept the floor with gold crosses swinging from their necks. I'm just a conservative evangelical Protestant from the mountains of North Carolina! From the beginning, I never felt like I really fit in with this crowd.

I struggled within myself, thinking that perhaps I should speak up. After all, God must have brought me here for a reason. But before I could make my decision, I saw my sister's hand pierce the air, and I remembered our conversation of the night before.

"Lord," I prayed, "grab hold of her tongue!"

The President saw Anne's hand, hesitated for a moment, and then called on her. He obviously knew who she was, and you could tell he was nervous. He stood with his arms folded across his chest, his chin resting on a finger, his head cocked down. I've never been trained to read a person's body language, but in this instance he looked as though he was preparing for an attack as he turned his face slightly away from Anne.

My sister stood up and introduced herself. "Mr. President, I'm Anne Graham Lotz." She then proceeded to give one of the most courageous and gracious yet challenging statements I have ever heard.

She began tactfully. "Mr. President, I would like to thank you for setting an example for the American people."

I thought, *What did she just say? Example?!*

As if reading my mind, Anne continued, "Mr. President, I want to thank you for going to church on Sunday and setting a positive example for others to follow." The President smiled. "I would also like to thank you, Mr. President," she said as she looked at him, "for carrying your Bible, God's Holy Word, publicly for all to see. I have heard that it has been quoted by you and that you have supported the right for every child to pray in school. Thank you, Mr. President."

Then Anne said, "Mr. President, the problem we have in the United States is a spiritual problem."

Here she goes, I thought. Then I comfortably sat back, knowing that she would make good.

"We cannot have a right relationship with our fellow man until we have a right relationship with God. Maybe the rabbi here would agree." She pointed to the man on her left, a chief rabbi from New York. He had a look of horror on his face, as if asking, *Why is she drawing me in on this?*

"Maybe the rabbi would concur, the place where we could all agree to begin would be God's Ten Commandments."

All of a sudden, the atmosphere in the room underwent a transformation—from stuffy and fuzzy to forthright and uncompromising. It started with an "amen," then a "that's right," then a "yes!" As Anne continued, heads nodded, verbal assents increased, even the rabbi nodded his head in consent. The President's face seemed to tighten as he sensed that he was losing control of his after-breakfast chat. Anne concluded her remarks with a strong and powerful challenge and a call to our nation's leaders to repent and walk with God and follow His commandments. Then she sat down in a hushed ballroom with all eyes on the President's response. There was none, and within a few short minutes, the meeting was over. People came up to me and said, "Franklin, you have some kind of sister."

"Thank you," I said, "I know that."

Even White House staffers came up to me and said, "Boy, Franklin, your sister is bold. You have to admire her."

Finally, I got Anne's attention. "Let's go," I said. As I looked around, I saw something that made me smile. Many people were waiting in line to get the President's autograph, but it appeared that there were more waiting to talk to my sister! Her gracious courage had inspired the nation's top religious leaders.

Anne nodded, politely excused herself, and gathered her coat. As we headed to the door the President saw us and quickly excused himself from the people who were standing in line waiting to see him.

"Anne," he said, "thank you for what you had to say. Franklin, good to see you again. Boy, your sister, she's something. She's some kind of lady, isn't she?"

The President was relying on more social programs, more volunteerism, and more bureaucratic laws to address our nation's problems, but Anne made it very clear that America's problem is a failure to walk in sync with God. She revealed the fact that until we get in step with God, there isn't a government or social program devised that will put our nation in a right standing with God. If we don't walk with God, we can't walk with man.

Anne has never run for a political office, but because she walks with God, she was able to display the moral integrity that wins respect and earns the right to be heard. She broke through the limits that hold us back when we should speak the truth.

The Impact of a Woman

I've come to realize that many women have certain strengths that men just don't have. Just as Queen Esther displayed a gutsy boldness to approach a king (Esther 5), so Anne displayed the courage to stand before the President—but in a way that didn't alienate him. She was gracious. She looked first for common ground, expressing her appreciation and sincerely thanking him for what he had done well.

This is a lesson that all of us can learn. When we want to express our views, the quickest way to turn someone off is to start blasting. People everywhere are drawn to gracious words. Pascal said: "Cold words freeze people, and hot words scorch them, and bitter words make them bitter, and wrathful words make them wrathful. Kind words also produce their image on men's souls. . . . they smooth, quiet, and comfort the hearer."

Anne's gracious but truthful words certainly stamped an image in the President's mind that day. I think of Proverbs 31:25, 26, 30: *"She is clothed with strength and dignity. . . . She speaks with wisdom; . . . charm is deceptive, and beauty is fleeting; but a woman who fears the Lord is to be praised"* (NIV). I was back in the White House a few weeks later when my father was asked to pray at the President's second inauguration. After the ceremony, we went to the Capitol for a luncheon with the Senate. As we greeted the President, he said to me, "Franklin, I sure enjoyed meeting your sister. She certainly knows how to speak eloquently, doesn't she?" The Bible is very clear about the influence of a faith-filled woman: *"The lips of the righteous know what is fitting"* (Proverbs 10:32 NIV).

I've been to the White House enough to know that it's a virtual assembly line of greetings. Who knows how many tens of thousands of people work their way through to get that all-elusive handshake with the President, but I know this one thing: He remembers one of them, my sister Anne, who simply but boldly said, "Mr. President," and shared a message that the Lord had given her for that moment.

12 GUTSY, WITTY, SASSY

ALCUTTA, INDIA, SEEMS DESIGNED to offend every human
sensibility. The British used to refer to Calcutta as the "Hell
Hole," and by Western standards it could certainly appear to be a little
bit of hell on earth. Bob Pierce used to say there is more human misery per square inch in Calcutta than in any other city in the world.

If you don't prepare yourself mentally and spiritually, and somehow summon nerves of steel, you'll never be able to make it through
a day in that city. Each time I set foot in its squalor, I catch myself
looking at my watch and thinking, *When's the next flight out of here?*

My indoctrination into Calcutta took place over twenty years
ago. As Bob Pierce and I walked down a street, I had a difficult time
looking into the eyes of people whose skin on their skeleton-thin
bodies looked so fragile that I felt certain they could be easily
pierced with a pencil eraser. Their clothes, if you could call them
that, looked like they would never survive washing, and even their
humble attempts at hygiene proved startling. I watched a man
relieve himself in a gutter, only to see half a block downstream a
man brushing his teeth in the same gutter.

The poverty in Calcutta is a death sentence, and every morning
a truck drives slowly through the city streets, picking up the dead.
They stack the corpses like a cord of wood, then take them down
to the river for burning.

It's a ghastly sight to watch those bodies burn. As soon as the stiff-ened corpses hit the flames, the muscles, sinews, and tendons con-tract, many times grotesquely lifting the bodies into a sitting position, as if the dead were rising in front of you. The flames begin licking and then blackening the corpses' skinny limbs. The fire consumes the hair first, then collapses the skin, until the body falls back over. It was a chilling sight.

Even their religious services can get gory. We passed the Kali Temple, and I watched a priest take a goat and put its head inside a makeshift guillotine. He then pulled on the goat's back legs, stretching the animal out, while another priest lifted a bloody ax and chopped the goat's head off, which rolled onto the ground, spewing blood at the priest's feet. The headless body flailed about for twenty or thirty seconds before finally falling still.

Though leprosy has been largely contained in the West, its grotesque presence is still written on the faces and bodies of count-less men, women, and children in Calcutta. You think you're watching a horror film when you see people walking around with a nose missing or half of the face eaten away. Others walk around with just one ear, and a pinkish-white cavern covers what should be the left half of their face. Besides leprosy, other skin conditions also thrive. The lack of hygiene and nutrition produces the most unsightly blotches, rashes, and skin diseases.

In short, as soon as you set foot in Calcutta, your senses—what you see, hear, smell, and feel—scream, *Let's get out of here.* It's almost beyond my imagination that someone would move from another country and purposefully seek out Calcutta as their home, but back in 1975, I met someone who had done just that.

The Strength of a Woman

Mother Teresa was holding a dying man as we arrived for a visit. We were told we'd have to wait; the Albanian nun was not about to leave a person who was near death simply to attend to some visiting Americans. I couldn't help but admire her. She knew her calling in life and made that her priority.

When I greeted Mother Teresa for the first time, I was moved by how fragile she seemed. That was in the early seventies. Her body was so tiny I wondered how she got along, but there was a strength in that woman that would put Arnold Schwarzenegger to shame.

Twenty years later, I found she hadn't changed one bit. She was still fragile and wrinkled, as she continued to exhibit an undeniable power. I was in Washington, D.C., when she spoke at the 1995 National Prayer Breakfast. She refused to sit at the head table. As a matter of fact, she refused to sit at any table. This indirect rebuke of the President's policies on abortion and her insistence on identifying with the poor made the entire world sit up and take notice.

When it came time for Mother Teresa to speak, the curtains parted and she walked in. She was so short that the lectern nearly covered her, leaving just her eyes and the top of her head in plain view. But nobody could deny they were listening to a woman of tremendous stature. The pro-abortion political leaders—including President Clinton and Attorney General Janet Reno—seemed to cringe when this gutsy woman urged us to respect and cherish all life. President Clinton looked like a son being lectured by his mother. I know that the President didn't agree with her, but he must have admired her strong conviction for what she believed was right.

Today, women who want to achieve are urged to seek political or financial power. I have no problem with a woman who feels called to run for office, seek a career, or even build her own business. What I do have a problem with is suggesting that these are the only routes to power. Mother Teresa points to a spiritual power and authority that government and business leaders can only dream about.

I had witnessed this same power long before I met Mother Teresa. This particular woman never ran for office, nor did she ever really work outside the home. Because of this, her accomplishments might be marginalized by the social engineers who want to remake our society; but like Mother Teresa, my mother, Ruth Bell Graham, showed me another example of the woman God uses.

The Warrior Wife

Ruth Bell Graham has been, most of the time, a stay-at-home mom. Nobody, though, should mistake her calling for lack of ambition and ability. If they do that, I'm telling you, they've got the wrong woman. In fact, in this day and age when the world puts pressure on women to get out into the workforce, it takes fortitude for a woman to stay home and raise her family.

In the mid-seventies, the city of Charlotte hosted a Billy Graham Day at which President Gerald Ford was scheduled to speak. In the wake of Watergate, political protesters were more common than houseflies, and they used any public gathering to vent their anger. This event was no different, and protesters were actually bused in from outside the area.

One hapless protester chose the wrong place to sit—right in front of my mother. His sign said Down with the Pigs, or something like that, and he kept waving it so that Mama's view of the platform was blocked.

He waved it once too often. He was about to find out the power of a woman of candor. Mama reached out and jerked the sign out of the protester's hand, then put it in a place where he couldn't touch it—she sat on it!

The protester was dumbfounded as he turned and looked at Mama sitting proud as a peacock. He thought he had chosen a seat in front of a timid, middle-aged woman, but now this "timid woman" was sitting on his sign and smiling in his direction!

"Can I have my sign back?" he asked in a gruff tone.

"Nope," Mama told him with a twinkle in her eye.

Rather indignant, he said, "Lady, I have a constitutional right to protest."

My mother grinned at him and cheerfully said, "Well, I have a constitutional right to see the President. When he is finished, you'll get your sign back."

The perplexed boy sat down in a stupor. Later he got the crazy idea of suing my mother for assault. Needless to say, it didn't get too far; the legal system had a difficult time believing that a small-framed woman in her fifties—and the wife of Billy Graham, no less—had assaulted a strong, long-haired hippie boy in his twenties. The case was eventually dropped. Even so, my mother refused to back down. "I'd rather go to jail," she said. And she would have—believe me.

THE STRENGTH OF MY FATHER'S SUCCESS

Daddy would be the first to say that Mama's strength is behind much of his success. She has written several books and magazine articles and found many of Daddy's sermon illustrations over the years. One book she wrote, *Legacy of a Pack Rat,* typifies her role of gathering quotes, ideas, and thoughts that Daddy could use in his sermons. Her life was consumed with helping my father become the man God called him to be, without compromising her duties to the family. And she still found time for writing. How did she get it all done?

It called for tremendous motivation on her part. Since Daddy was gone so much, Mama was determined that what little time he had at home would be restful. She protected him from household problems, taking care of them in advance so that he could spend time with us kids when he returned, rather than having to fix a dripping faucet or a leaky roof. She also took care of the discipline—Mama didn't want us to dread Daddy's return, so she dished out the proper punishment on the spot.

One of the special burdens Mama faced was being married to a public person. Every public personality is considered fair game to be ridiculed, exposed, or talked negatively about. In fact, a book was published attacking Mother Teresa before her death. Though Daddy is now universally respected and well thought of, there were times when Christians and non-Christians alike personally and viciously attacked him.

Mama did her part by simply hiding the paper from Daddy. "That's just nonsense," she'd say after reading a malicious article. "That person doesn't know what they're talking about," and she'd remove all evidence of the attack. She realized that there would be no benefit for my father to read false, often ridiculous charges, so she focused on making our home a haven of rest for Daddy.

I'm convinced that one of the reasons my father continues to preach long after most of his peers have retired is because he married a woman who allowed him to minister with such freedom.

But my mother's ministry was by no means limited to my father. Our house was a serene refuge to many runaway kids on drugs, women facing difficult times in their marriages, people needing food or consolation. Mama opened her arms and her home to all of them, fed them, and frequently offered them a bed. And she did so with tenacity. Mama gave herself 100 percent to the hurting; she didn't hold back at all.

My mother has an infectious sense of humor and wit, and a sharp mind that will outfox the best of them. Her eyes are always sparkling—I think she was born with a sense of adventure and mischief. Yet by today's standards, some people might look at my mother's life—supporting her husband, raising her children, caring for the needy—and think she restricted herself. As a young girl, my mother gave up her dream to serve God as a missionary to Tibet in order to become the wife of an evangelist who would almost never be home. Though she has been a very successful author and a great public speaker, she never owned her own business, engaged in a career, or ran for office—but I've met few women who have made the impact that my mother has made. I think even today that she would say that her greatest joy has been raising five children and supporting her husband.

You see, the key to living life beyond the limits is to serve God in whatever situation He has called you. Paul writes in 1 Corinthians 7:17: "*Each one should retain the place in life that the Lord assigned to him and to which God has called him*" (NIV).

After all, isn't that what Jesus did? He sacrificed His life so that we could be what God wanted us to be—sinners forgiven by His grace and walking in sync with Him.

There's another woman who typifies sacrificial living whom God called out of Australia. A single nurse. God is definitely more creative than the feminists. He doesn't define success along one, narrow path. His calling extends to women from all walks of life and with all sorts of abilities.

A WOMAN ENTERS A MAN'S WORLD

As a young woman growing up in Bundaberg, New South Wales, Australia, Aileen Coleman caught the eye of many a young man. She is a tall, attractive woman with a sassy sense of humor, and she is every inch a lady. She had several marriage proposals over the years, but she turned them all down. Aileen knew God had called her to take the gospel of Jesus Christ to the Bedouin, the nomadic tribes of the Middle East. This was during an age when few women were interested in living and working in that part of the world.

The desert is a harsh place to live. It is dirty, with swarming hordes of flies almost to biblical plague proportions that engulf and pester anyone who travels through at certain times of the year. Temperatures can soar to 120 degrees Fahrenheit.

It is also, by all accounts, a man's world where nomads travel the desert almost as they did thousands of years ago, living in their black tents made of goat hair, tending their herds of camels, sheep, and goats. The faith of these nomads is Islam, and women in the Islamic world have very few rights and not a whole lot of social standing. As a medical professional, had Aileen remained in her native Australia, she would have received a lifetime of esteem and respect, but she willingly gave all that up to live as a woman in the Arab world.

Her mission mirrors that of many of the Lord's servants, as it must for all of us if we are to stay in sync with God. In heaven, Jesus received all the glory and praise that was due to Him, but because His Father wanted to save us from our sins, Jesus willingly left that place of affirmation and glory and came to this earth to take the sins of this world, and to offer His life as a ransom for many. *"For you know the grace of our Lord Jesus Christ, that though He was rich, yet for your sakes He became poor, that you through His poverty might become rich"* (2 Cor. 8:9).

God has a sense of humor. Leave it to God to send a woman into a man's world to be His ambassador. Leave it to God to send a single person to reach out to the extended families of the Bedouin. Leave it to God to lead an educated, sophisticated lady to bring the truth to unschooled nomads, but God did it, and what an impact it has made.

Boy, has it ever. When Aileen first began her ministry to the Bedouin in the late fifties, she teamed up with Dr. Eleanor Soltau, a physician whose specialty is in chest diseases. Dr. Soltau knew a lot about tuberculosis. At a young age, she had contracted TB herself and had a lung removed due to this disease.

We talked earlier about how God can use even the most harrowing situations for His glory. Dr. Soltau, also single, learned this lesson very well. Tuberculosis runs rampant among the Bedouin. In the late fifties, before Aileen and Eleanor opened their clinic, the Bedouin people were dying by the thousands because there was no place they could go for treatment of TB. Instead of making excuses—"I only have one lung, Lord, surely you don't want me to go to a dirty, dusty culture!"—Eleanor walked with God in obedience and let Him use her own past difficulties for His great future plans.

Eleanor, like Aileen, was tall and striking, and she shared Aileen's love for the people of the Middle East. Together, these two women established a unique mission hospital in Northern Jordan known as the Annoor Sanatorium, outside of the desert oasis of Mafraq, and began treating TB patients.

In the mid-sixties, there were few known believers among the Bedouin tribes of the Middle East; today, there is at least one believer in every tribe. Whether you search in Iraq, Jordan, Syria, Saudi Arabia, or Lebanon, you can find a Bedouin believer, in large part, because of Aileen and Eleanor's ministry to care for the sick. Their work continues to this day.

As patients recover from their ailments, Aileen and her nursing staff teach them Scripture, which they put to Bedouin tunes. Aileen holds voluntary services at the hospital at 6:00 P.M. each day; therefore, the Bedouin decided that 6:00 must be the proper time for Christians to pray! A Bedouin man, after spending four months in the sanatorium, returned to tell Aileen how Jesus had saved him from the despair of a wandering life in which he could never really know where he stood with God.

The Bedouin live in extended family tents, so when one member emerges as a believer in Jesus Christ with his heart full of songs, everybody soon hears about it.

One particular man became very ill and decided to seek the services of Annoor Sanatorium. He didn't know how to find the hospital, but his uncle, who had been there as a patient, assured him, "Jesus will help you find the way."

The young man reached the Syrian/Jordanian border looking very much like what he was—a poor, dirty, and very sick Bedouin man. He prayed, "God, my uncle told me Jesus would help me find the way. I don't know where to go."

A taxi driver saw the forlorn man and pulled over, asking him, "Are you trying to find the hospital?"

"Yes!" the man exclaimed with astonishment

God does answer prayer, if prayed by faith believing, whether from you or from a Bedouin tribesman. The Lord Jesus guided this man's footsteps and the taxi driver took him right to the hospital's front gate.

Courageously obedient, Aileen and Eleanor have seen prayer like this answered over and over again as they have faithfully served God in this remote part of the world. I don't use that word *courageous* lightly. Aileen has grit. Maybe you know someone like that. After the 1967 war with Israel, known as the Six-Day War, Jordan lost much of its army. Iraq moved several of its army divisions into Jordan to protect it from what the Iraqis called "any further Israeli aggression." At the same time, the PLO began training its own army, which tried to overthrow King Hussein several years later. This became known as Black September.

The PLO established a terrorist training camp in Mafraq, which threatened the local people, holding them to martial law and strict curfews. During this era, there was a tragic accident in Mafraq in which a roof collapsed, partially burying a woman under the rubble. The locals sent someone to find Aileen, asking her to come as soon as possible lest the woman die.

It was dark, but Aileen drove through Mafraq's narrow dirt streets to tend to this woman. Along the way, she was stopped by a PLO roadblock. She rolled down her window, and the machine gun-toting soldiers saw she was a Westerner. (The PLO assumes that all Westerners are enemies of their people.) The fact that Aileen was rushing to save the life of an Arab woman didn't matter to them.

"You have broken curfew," one soldier growled. "We're going to kill you."

Without flinching, Aileen looked the soldier square in the face and said, "If you're going to shoot me, you better do it quick because I'm in a hurry and have to go." She stepped on the gas pedal and sped away, leaving a stunned group of gaping soldiers behind in gas fumes. They had never encountered a woman quite like Aileen.

A Different Standard

Obviously today's popular magazines haven't seen anyone like Aileen either. They exhort their readers to lavish themselves by pursuing external gratification: beauty, sex, money, possessions, and an active night life.

While women were marching to increase their freedoms, Aileen willingly risked hers. "I could never get inside the Arab world as an evangelist," she admits. "If I tried, I'd be out on the next plane—unless I was thrown in prison instead."

Aileen found a more profound and lasting pleasure, and in doing so, broke through the barriers that would have been seen by others as detour signs. Being a female from the West and living in the male-dominated Middle East would intimidate most, but not Aileen Coleman. Her unshakable faith has even taken her beyond the barrel of a terrorist machine gun.

Those same magazines purchased at the supermarket checkout stands tout the glory of "successful" and "happy" living. They've completely forgotten that mankind has already been there and done that. Remember Adam and Eve? Their lives and environment defined everything good in life—but they weren't satisfied. They just had to go tinkering around where they didn't belong.

God hasn't called us to be happy according to the world's standards. He's called us to be faithful. We may not be happy about our calling at first, but if we are obedient, true happiness will often follow. Too many people today think they can disobey God's laws and commands simply because they're not happy. What does happiness have to do with it?

Do you think Noah was happy building a boat on dry land while everybody laughed at him for a hundred years? But he kept driving those nails.

Do you think Jesus was happy when His Father told Him, "I'm going to send you to earth"?

"You mean that little planet on the other side of the Milky Way?"

Do you think Jesus was happy about the cross? He prayed three times in the Garden of Gethsemane—"Lord, if it be thy will, take this cup from me." But it wasn't God's will, and Jesus was obedient unto death.

This search for happiness can knock us out of sync with God. As the life of Jesus makes clear, keeping in sync with God is about *obedience*. Any other pursuit will get in the way.

Everywhere, people are working themselves to death trying to achieve the symbols of success—an expensive car, a power suit, and a beautiful home. Aileen can't point to any of these. In fact, she can't even point to large numbers of converts. Many might dare to call her life wasted, caring for the physical needs of dirty, sick tribal people of the Middle East. But Aileen has discovered that being obedient leads to something even more profound than happiness—lasting joy.

The Bible tells us,

People who want to get rich fall into temptation and a trap and into many foolish and harmful desires that plunge men into ruin and destruction. . . . Flee from all of this, and pursue righteousness, godliness, faith, love, endurance and gentleness. Fight the good fight of the faith. Take hold of the eternal life to which you were called when you made your good confession. (1 Tim. 6:9, 11–12 NIV)

The Bible's view of happiness is quite different from the world's. Happy are those who find *wisdom* (Prov. 3:13); we certainly don't see that glaring across a magazine cover! Happy are those who have *mercy* on the poor (Prov. 14:21). Happy are those who are *reproached* for the name of Christ (1 Peter 4:14). Happy are those who *endure* (James 5:11). Finally, happy are those *whose God is the Lord* (Ps. 144:15). This is an accurate portrayal of Aileen Coleman.

"As long as I have life," Aileen adds, "I'm ready to preach the gospel." Why? When Jesus sent out the disciples two by two, He sent them *"to preach the kingdom of God and to heal the sick"* (Luke 9:2).

WHEN A WOMAN WALKS WITH GOD

Many women embrace a life that goes against the grain of our modern society. They have in common a shared faith in God, an ironclad commitment to serve Jesus Christ, and a daily practice of learning to walk in obedience with the King of kings and the Lord of lords: This is accomplished through the careful study of God's Word while applying it to their daily lives.

In short, their strength is in their unselfishness and their simple faith to believe God and obey. Someone once said that the most difficult lesson for young people to learn is this: When you're trying to make an impression, that is the impression you make. So many women today are trying to make a name for themselves by impressing society that they can have it all, do it all, or buy it all. But women like Aileen and Eleanor gave it all away. They came to the Cross with open hands.

Yet each one of them would testify to a rich, meaningful, and rewarding life. Each one would tell you she's gained far more than she has ever sacrificed. Each one is a testimony to the truth of Christ's words, *"For whoever desires to save his life will lose it, but whoever loses his life for My sake will find it"* (Matt. 16:25).

In a world full of religions that demean women—leaving them with little respect and virtually no rights—Christianity stands alone in affirming the dignity, calling, and capability of women in all walks of life. In spite of what the world says, the greatest calling for a woman is the responsibility of raising her children and managing a home. Our country is in a mess in part because of the fact that we have failed to teach our children a value system, which begins in the home. For those women in the workplace or in a professional career, your calling is great if you are where God has placed you.

If you want to be a woman of God, obey Him. Don't litter your mind with all the garbage that is cast in front of you by the world: tabloid magazines and talk shows that fling gossip, scandal, and slander around for all to hear. Remember *garbage in, garbage out.*

Instead of keeping in step with Hollywood, change your direction and walk with God. How? Talk to Him. Ask Him to take your hand and lead you through each day of your life so that you stay on track. Study His Word—and obey it.

But you say, "I've tried and failed." Tell *Him.* He was here on earth. He understands. *"To this you were called, because Christ suffered for you, leaving you an example, that you should follow in his steps"* (1 Peter 2:21 NIV).

When the religious leaders caught a young woman in an act of adultery and dragged her before Jesus, they knew (as did Jesus) that under the law, this woman could have been stoned. Instead of condemning her, however, Jesus knelt down and wrote something in the sand. Then He stood up and said, *"He who is without sin among you, let him throw a stone at her first"* (John 8:7).

One by one the men slipped quietly from the crowd. When all had left, Jesus asked the woman, "Where are your accusers?"

"Lord, they're gone."

Jesus answered, *"Neither do I condemn you; go and sin no more"* (John 8:11).

Sin limits us and holds us back. Jesus forgave a woman who was filled with demons and He set her free. He forgave a woman caught in adultery and He set her free. He'll set you free, but you have to be willing to obey. The book of James tells us to *"submit yourselves, then, to God. Resist the devil, and he will flee from you. Come near to God and he will come near to you"* (4:7–8 NIV). If we fill our minds with things of the world, we will continually be defeated. If we want to be in sync with God, we need to redirect our thoughts in obedience to Him. This is the path we must follow—to set our minds on the things in heaven, not on the things on earth (Col. 3:2).

13

THE DOC AND THE MOB'S LAWYER

GOD KNOWS HOW TO CLEAR the way to make room for His big adventures. We've seen that God can take men, women, and children beyond their human limits for His glory. In the next two chapters, we're going to see how God can use a change of schedule and even disaster to accomplish His will and His purpose. If we're obedient, God will allow us to walk with Him, and He'll lead us down roads, through valleys, over mountains, and into experiences that we could never have dreamed possible.

That's certainly what happened in the life of Dr. Richard Furman, a general and thoracic (chest) surgeon who, with his brother Dr. Lowell Furman, helped me found World Medical Mission. Every year, Dick and Lowell travel around the world to volunteer their medical services in the name of Jesus Christ.

In 1978 Dick, his wife, Harriet, and their three children were on their way to Kenya in East Africa via New York and then London. There was a delay in their flight from North Carolina into New York, so they missed their international connection. Dick checked out several other airlines but couldn't find another flight into London with five available seats.

He looked at his watch. It was ten minutes before midnight, so Dick and his family prepared to spend the night in a hotel. As the family began to gather their things, Dick walked back to the counter to check one more possibility.

Standing at the TWA counter, Dick questioned the ticket agent and received the response he was looking for. "Yes, Dr. Furman, we do have one last flight going out, but it leaves in ten minutes. I don't think you can make it."

Dick looked behind him. Harriet was standing there with three kids and a mound of luggage. Was it possible to move all that luggage a half mile in ten minutes? Only if they got a cab.

Dick, who never gets in a real hurry, informed Harriet of the change in plans and then darted outside to hail a taxi. "I need to get to the next terminal!" he said.

"No way, buddy, I'm not about to take you just to the next terminal," the driver told him.

"Why not?"

"I've been sitting here an hour. I'm going to wait for somebody who is going to Manhattan."

"How about if I pay a Manhattan fare?"

"It'll cost you thirty-seven bucks."

"Thirty-seven dollars to go to the next terminal?"

"That's right. Take it or leave it," he snapped.

"Okay, I'll do it." Dick knew he was being robbed, but he had no choice.

Dick waved his family into the cab. The taxi took off and stopped less than a half mile away. The Furmans grabbed their luggage and raced through security and then to their gate.

The door was closed.

Dick's heart sank.

"Are you trying to catch this flight?" an airline agent asked.

"Yes," Dick said.

"I don't think they've pushed back, yet. Let me see what I can do." She got on the phone, nodded toward Dick and his family, then rushed toward the Jetway, motioning them to board.

"We can board you, though none of the seats are together. We'll have to check your luggage. Just leave it here."

When Dick arrived in London, he called me. I picked up the phone in the middle of the night and heard his familiar voice. "Franklin, I'm going to be late. We missed a connection and it threw the whole trip off. Call Nairobi and tell them we won't be on our scheduled flight."

I was back to sleep almost before I had hung up the receiver. When I woke the next morning, Dick's call seemed only a dream. Later that day, I received a call from our friends in Nairobi.

"Where's Dick?" they wanted to know. "He didn't show up."

At first I had no earthly idea what could have happened to him. As we talked on, I began to recall Dick's midnight message. I started laughing and then told the hospital about Dick's delay.

I hung up the phone, not realizing that God had divinely intervened and redirected Dick's steps in order to keep an appointment He had made with one of Vegas's high rollers. After Dick boarded the plane and got his family situated, he was so exhausted from the ordeal that he went right to sleep. The plane had been in the air not more than two or three hours. The cabin lights were turned off, and most passengers were asleep. From the flight deck an announcement broke through the quiet stillness. "Is there a doctor on board?"

Dick rubbed the sleep out of his eyes, went forward, identified himself, and was led into the first-class cabin. A well-dressed, elderly man was very ill. The flight attendants had removed his suit coat and laid him out on the floor.

The man was still conscious. "My name is Dr. Richard Furman," he told the man. "I'm a surgeon. Can you tell me what the problem is?"

"Chest pain," the man whispered.

"Was it sudden?" Dick asked.

"Yes."

"Have you had any history of heart trouble?"

"Yes."

The man's face was ashen. Rivers of perspiration ran down his forehead. Dick reached out to check the man's pulse from the neck first, then moved down to the man's wrist. The man's skin was clammy, and the pulse was very weak and irregular.

Clearly, the man was having a heart attack.

Dick determined that the main threat to this man's life came from the fact that the blocked arteries of his heart were choking the blood flow to the heart muscle. These arteries had to be opened immediately or he would die.

Dick turned to the flight attendant. "Get me some oxygen and collect all the nitroglycerin tablets you can get from the passengers." An announcement blared through the speakers throughout each section of the plane, and the tablets were gathered from many travelers who suffered with heart disease themselves.

Dick placed several pills under the man's tongue, waited for them to dissolve, then gave him some more.

Conversation stopped. Dick turned the oxygen to full flow and continued to place the nitroglycerin tablets under the man's tongue in hopes that the heart's arteries would open enough to carry the oxygen to the muscle.

Dick had no idea what time it was or how long the plane had been up in the air. He could only hope that they were nearing London so the patient could be taken to the nearest hospital. He asked the steward if he could speak to one of the pilots concerning the man's condition.

Within minutes, the captain came into the cabin. "We're ten minutes from the halfway mark," he said. "We can stay on schedule to London unless you think ten minutes will make a difference."

Dick said, "Medically speaking, the quicker we get him on the ground, the better his chances. This man could die anytime."

The captain didn't say anything. He simply turned and went back to the cockpit. A few moments later, Dick felt the plane take a sharp turn to the left. The pilot headed to Nova Scotia and contacted a hospital there.

Dick kept checking the man's pulse. He'd periodically talk to the man, just to make sure he was still conscious, but by this time his patient could do little more than nod.

"We're getting you down," Dick told him. "Your pulse is weak, but the nitroglycerin seems to be working, you're doing fine."

Dick stayed with the passenger throughout the flight. "Dr. Furman," the steward informed, "we'll be landing in about an hour." Thirty minutes later, the elderly man collapsed into another episode of chest pain, weak pulse, and an irregular rhythm. He was having a second heart attack. He quit responding to Dick's comments.

Dick felt like his hands were tied. He didn't have any of the equipment that he needed; he couldn't even check the man's blood pressure. It was like being back in his medical school days, trying to guess what was going on.

The only medical treatment available was oxygen and nitroglycerin. He knew that was the man's only chance. As soon as one tablet dissolved, he placed another one under the man's tongue.

Ten minutes later, the patient rallied. Dick noticed a stronger pulse, and the man began to respond once again to his questions.

It was an exhausting hour, but finally the plane landed, and Dick helped put the man on the stretcher and stayed with him until he was safely placed in the ambulance, more to reassure him than anything else.

"You're being taken to the emergency room at the hospital," Dick explained. "You're not being abandoned. You're doing well right now—that's a real good sign."

The man whispered to one of the attendants to give him his coat. He pulled out a business card and handed it to Dick, thanking him for his help. When Dick reboarded the plane, he looked at the card and discovered that the man he had helped was Morris Shenker.

Unbeknownst to Dick at that time, Morris Shenker was one of Vegas's most well-known citizens according to *Life* magazine in 1968. He served as Jimmy Hoffa's chief counsel and was known as the mob's lawyer. He had gone to Vegas in the forties and worked himself up to chairman of the board and CEO of the famed Dunes Hotel and Casino in the neon capital of the world.

While serving in the African mission hospital over the next five weeks, Dick couldn't help but wonder about the outcome of Morris Shenker. Because of the man's age, Dick was uncertain about his chance of survival. In the mid-seventies, communication wasn't nearly as convenient as it is now—especially when trying to communicate from a remote bush hospital.

A few weeks into Dick's stay in Nairobi, I was in Africa myself and went by to see the Furmans and visit with the missionaries at the hospital. When Dick told about his encounter with Mr. Shenker, I encouraged him to call when he got back to the States to find out how he was doing. In my opinion, Dick hadn't been diverted for no reason at all.

Dick responded, "Why don't you call him?"

"Why would I call him? I don't have any connection with him. You're the one who saved his life—not me!"

"All right," Dick said, "I'll call."

When we got back, I went over to Dick's office and sat across from him as he placed a call to the Dunes Hotel.

"May I ask why you need to speak with Mr. Shenker?" the receptionist asked.

"I'm a doctor; I treated Mr. Shenker on an airplane a few weeks ago. I just wanted to find out how he was doing."

"Please hold."

Before Dick knew it, he had been transferred to an attorney, obviously a very suspicious one. He apparently thought Dick was calling to ask for payment, or something in return for his services. Dick explained that he didn't want anything, he was just anxious to find out about Mr. Shenker's physical condition. When the man was convinced of Dick's sincere inquiry, his tone softened.

"Mr. Shenker is doing very, very well," the lawyer explained. "He had bypass surgery and is recovering nicely."

We learned that Mr. Shenker had suffered a ventricular aneurism, which knocked out a big part of his heart. After Dick left him in Nova Scotia, a private jet transported him from Newfoundland to St. Louis, where he was treated by a world-renowned specialist. The attorney expressed appreciation to Dick for the care he had given to Mr. Shenker. "Had the plane continued to London," the lawyer explained, "Mr. Shenker wouldn't have been able to receive the services of the specialist in St. Louis, and he might not have recovered."

"I'm glad to hear that," Dick said. "Please give him my best wishes for a full recovery."

"Mr. Shenker will appreciate the fact that you called."

A few weeks later, Morris Shenker sent Dick a little gift and then called him. With a thick European accent, he invited Dick to come to Las Vegas as his guest. Dick replied that he didn't want anything, didn't expect anything, but felt it was very medically rewarding that a patient who had been so fragile and so close to death had pulled through and survived.

From then on, Dick would get calls in the middle of the night, as late as 2:00 or 3:00 in the morning. Morris Shenker just wanted to talk. He was very grateful to Dick and, as a result, always expressed interest in what Dick was doing. Many times he felt his day wasn't complete until he checked in with Dick. He continued extending invitations for Dick to visit him in Las Vegas.

"Well, Morris," Dick explained, "I don't gamble, but I would like to see you. Why don't you come to Boone? It's also a resort area, though a bit more quiet than Vegas. It's real cool in the summer."

Being accustomed to the bright lights of sin-city, Boone sounded safely mundane. Maybe that's why Mr. Shenker never arrived.

When Dick learned that my father was going to have a crusade in Nevada, he surprised Mr. Shenker one day by saying, "I'll tell you what. I'll come out during the Billy Graham crusade if you'll promise to go with me each night."

"All right, Dick," he responded. "That's a deal."

Dick told Mr. Shenker that Jane Austin and I would be in Las Vegas for the crusade and asked if it would be okay if we joined them. He graciously agreed, and when we arrived, he rolled out the red carpet. He even made a contribution to what he kept calling "the revival."

"GOD WON'T LET ME GO TO HELL"

The first day of a crusade is always busy. Dick and I didn't see Mr. Shenker until that night. By the time the meeting started, both Dick and I were up on the platform wondering where he was. Nearly a half hour into the meeting, we spotted him walking down the center aisle of the packed coliseum, finally settling in a seat on the third row. Dick and I looked at each other, astonished that he could find a perfect seat long after the meeting was underway.

At the conclusion of the service, we met Mr. Shenker and his wife for dinner. We shared backgrounds with each other and learned that he was Jewish. He startled us when out of the blue he asked, "Does nudity bother you?"

"What?" I asked, thinking I had surely misunderstood.

"I can get you front-row tickets to our show—the girls are nude."

"Well, Mr. Shenker," clearing my throat and looking over at Dick, "thank you very much for the invitation, but that's not something we would want to watch. I hope you understand."

He stared off into space for a moment, then said reluctantly, "Oh . . . well, maybe I can find something else."

As I thought about his question later that night, it seemed even more surprising that a man with an obviously diverse set of values would accept our invitation to come and hear Billy Graham, yet not be offended that we would decline his invitation. This was an amazing friendship. What made it possible? A physician had missed an airline connection, been rerouted to Mr. Shenker's flight, and ended up saving his life. I'll never be convinced that Dick's thwarted plans were an accident.

The Bible says, "'*My thoughts are not your thoughts, neither are your ways my ways,' declares the LORD*" (Isa. 55:8 NIV).

Dick knew the Lord had used him on the plane that night, and he wanted to be faithful to proclaim the gospel to this man who needed Christ. Dick steered the conversation back to spiritual matters. He shared with Mr. Shenker that perhaps God had given him a second chance to reconsider how he should spend the remaining years of his life.

Mr. Shenker was far from convicted. "I'm okay," he said. "I've given money to the revival. I send food to the needy. I'm a good person. God won't let me go to hell."

THE SWAN ROOM

The next morning, Dick talked to my father and asked him to sign a Bible for Mr. Shenker. When he did, he inscribed two verses:

> But we are all like an unclean thing, and all our right-eousnesses are like filthy rags; we all fade as a leaf, and our iniquities, like the wind, have taken us away. (Isa. 64:6)

> Jesus said to him, "I am the way, the truth, and the life. No one comes to the Father except through Me." (John 14:6)

The next night, Morris Shenker invited us to join him for dinner in the Swan Room, the formal restaurant in the Dunes Hotel. In the middle of the room was a harpist seated on a beautifully constructed swan floating on the water.

The hotel was ornate. The walls looked like marble, but touching them revealed only plastic—deceptive, like a Hollywood movie set. With the exception of those at our table, there didn't appear to be anyone in that dining room younger than seventy.

For an old country boy like me, and for the Furmans from deep down in Georgia, we had never seen anything like Las Vegas—it was one gaudy town. And Mr. Shenker seemed to love its flamboyant flair.

Dick noticed the evening slipping by; he didn't want to miss what might be his last chance. He looked Mr. Shenker in the eye and said, "Morris, you came very close to death on the plane many months ago. What this crusade out here with Billy Graham is all about is to explain that all the good that we do in this life is not a guarantee that we'll get into heaven."

Dick took out the Bible and presented it to Mr. Shenker. The lawyer's eyes widened when they fell on my father's signature. "I want you to realize what Billy Graham is saying," Dick pointed to the Scriptures. "Your good deeds are not going to get you into heaven. As a physician, what I did to help you was a small thing; the surgeon who operated on your heart also played a small part in sustaining your life, but it was the Lord who brought you through.

"I can't give you that everlasting life," Dick said. "Nor can the surgeon in St. Louis. Only God, the Great Physician, who sent the Messiah, His Son, Jesus Christ, can give you eternal life."

Mr. Shenker listened intently. The conversation seemed to disturb him. Dick was beginning to get through, but Mr. Shenker was restless. At the first opportunity, he changed the subject. "Thank you, Dick, thank you very much for the book. Please, thank Dr. Graham. I appreciate so much all that you have done for me."

AN INVITATION

Mr. Shenker attended the crusade the next night as he had promised, and this time he brought his family and some friends visiting from St. Louis. When my father gave the invitation to come to Jesus Christ by faith, Mr. Shenker looked like he was sitting on hot coals, shifting from side to side. He seemed amazed, later, as his friends from St. Louis got up and went forward to receive Christ as their Lord and Savior. He didn't know what to make of it.

Morris Shenker certainly heard the gospel more than once that week. After our visit Dick would drop him a note from time to time. "I'm still praying for you," Dick would say. "I hope everything is coming along."

Then, one Christmas, Dick didn't hear from him. It had been an unusually long time since he had received a late-night phone call, so he contacted Mr. Shenker's secretary to check up on him. Dick was told that Mr. Shenker had died.

GOD KNOWS THE OUTCOME

Things don't happen by chance when you give God room to work in your life. God allowed a set of circumstances to position Dick on the same plane with Mr. Shenker. God knew that Billy Graham would be holding a crusade in Las Vegas. None of that was by chance. I don't know what commitment Mr. Shenker made, if any, before his death a few years later. He heard the truth and was given the wonderful opportunity for eternal life, and Dick Furman was faithful to his calling that night on the Boeing 747.

Many who attended my father's crusade in Las Vegas responded to the invitation to accept Christ, joining Mr. Shenker's friends from St. Louis who went forward that night. God even used Morris Shenker to bring them to Christ. Perhaps they would have never considered attending an evangelistic crusade had Morris Shenker not invited them. Who knows, maybe in the last few minutes of his life, Mr. Shenker remembered those verses my father had written in his Bible. Perhaps Dick Furman's words came to mind, and, in the privacy of his own deathbed, Morris accepted Jesus Christ into his heart.

Something like this would be impossible to orchestrate. Being a part of it all is where life gets fun for the believer. A good friend of mine, Tommy Coomes, is one of the fathers of today's contemporary Christian music and a founder of Maranatha! Music. In the early seventies, he led a group known as Love Song. Several years ago, Tommy wrote a song about a man whose life was headed for disaster, but after he turned the driving over to the "chief," he's now in the "backseat," and God is in the front seat at the wheel of life.

It's a thrill to sit back and let God do the driving, taking us through the rugged terrain of life. Our God is a creative God, and He finds ways to lead us into situations that we could never get into on our own.

With God directing my path, I discover a new element in everyday living: The people I meet and the situations I find myself thrown into become full of new opportunities. God's got me here for a reason, so I sit back and watch His Spirit move. I let God be my appointment secretary. I never imagine that I'm somewhere by accident. Just in case God's behind it, I want to be ready.

To the world, adventure is found in the amusement rides of Walt Disney World, the game tables and shows of Las Vegas, or an around-the-world cruise. But these activities inevitably lead to the attitude, "Been there, done that, bought the T-shirt, now what?" Because these things are superficial, there's a big letdown at the end of the rainbow. The amusements become only diversions to an empty life. They never satisfy. That's when people start searching for something more.

Well, let me tell you that walking in sync with God never gets old. The next time you find yourself sitting next to someone on a plane or on public transit during your morning commute, don't assume that it's by chance; consider the possibility that God has strategically placed you there. As 1 Peter 3:15 says, *"Always be prepared to give an answer to everyone who asks you to give the reason for the hope that you have"* (NIV).

FLAMES IN VEGAS

14

To MANY PEOPLE, Las Vegas is the equivalent of a modern day Sodom and Gomorrah, deserving of God's judgment with fire from heaven. God warned Sodom and Gomorrah of coming judgment if its people did not repent (Genesis 19). One thing that I have appreciated about my father is that over the years he has been willing to go anywhere at any time to preach the gospel. So when he received an invitation from the few churches in Las Vegas to come and hold a crusade meeting, he quickly accepted.

I had gone to Vegas with Dick Furman to attend my father's 1978 crusade. I was scheduled to fly to California for meetings and planned to be back in time for the opening night of my father's crusade. I got dressed and slipped downstairs for an early breakfast when I noticed a waitress looking with horror out the window.

"What's going on?" I asked.

"I think the MGM Hotel is on fire."

When I looked outside, there was a column of dark, black smoke and flames billowing out of the MGM.

"How long has it been burning?" I asked.

"I'm not sure. I just noticed it."

I called my father immediately. He was still asleep, and it took him a few minutes to answer the phone. He couldn't imagine why I would call at such an early hour.

"Daddy," I explained, "the MGM Hotel across the street is on fire. Thought you'd want to know."

As soon as I hung up, I ran to Dick Furman's room and knocked until he rallied.

"Dick, the MGM's on fire," I said, as he cracked the door open. "Look out your window—I gotta go—be back later."

I had no idea at that time what would unfold throughout the day. Dick quickly got dressed and went outside to get a better view. I hurried to catch my flight. Only a few of the rescue and fire trucks had arrived. There was total chaos and confusion. It seemed as though the entire hotel was engulfed in flames. People were screaming and using chairs to bust the windows, sending glass splinters onto the sidewalk below. The falling glass became so dangerous that the rescue workers had to retreat several times to keep from getting cut to pieces themselves. The MGM Hotel was one of Las Vegas's highest skyscrapers, so falling glass from top floors picked up a lethal speed by the time it hit the ground.

Dick was shaken by the thousands of wailing cries and high-pitched screams. The Bible tells us that is what hell will be like. Can you imagine an eternity filled with never-ending terror?

As Dick drew closer to the scene, he saw people hanging off the balconies hundreds of feet above the ground. There was widespread panic. People on the ground were horrified; those trapped inside were frightened to the point of hysteria.

Dick saw the firemen scurry with the ladders, rescuing one person, climbing down, then going back up again. There was so much going on it was hard to take it all in with one glance. Smoke bellowed from the hundreds of occupied hotel rooms. But the ladders could not reach to the highest floors.

These people are never going to make it, Dick thought to himself. *They'll never get everybody out of there at this rate.*

There were not enough ambulances and EMTs (emergency

medical technicians) to handle the pandemonium. Dick spotted a policeman and yelled, "I'm a doctor. Can I help?"

The officer ran toward him, pointing in the right direction. "We've set up a medical crew on the far corner around the building."

"Hold on," a rescue worker cut in. "We don't have a doctor here; we sure could use your help."

Dick nodded and rolled up his sleeves to help the EMTs set up an emergency care center in the parking lot immediately in front of the hotel. The wind had shifted, and the smoke grew so thick on the other side of the building that the firemen couldn't take the victims to the main emergency station. For almost two hours, 90 percent of the rescuers brought all their victims to the secondary center where Dick had taken charge.

People were pouring out of the hotel, coughing and spilling onto the ground. Many unconscious victims were brought in draped over the arms and shoulders of firemen. The first patient Dick saw was a Caucasian man whose face was black from soot. *He's not gonna make it*, Dick thought. *He can't breathe.*

"Get me a laryngoscope!" Dick yelled. He put an endotracheal tube down the man's windpipe and started administering oxygen, and the man started breathing again.

"Just keep the tubes coming," he instructed the technician. At one point, he got so busy that he just stuck a handful of endotracheal tubes in his pocket. All he had time to do was to intubate the patients and then turn them over to an EMT to bag breathe the victims with oxygen. There was no time or personnel to perform lifesaving heroics on patients who weren't going to make it. The injured kept flooding in for hours. Stretchers were set up for those who were recovering.

One of the victims carried in was a young woman in her midthirties. She was attractive, probably no more than five feet tall, and looked as if she could have been an athlete. *It's a good thing she appears to be in good shape,* Dick thought. *It might help pull her through.*

"Put her on a stretcher," he shouted, and then he suctioned out the bits of smoke and black carbon that had filled her lungs, inserted an endotracheal tube, and started monitoring her blood pressure.

Out of the corner of his eye, Dick saw a huge, burly man charging his way. Officials had marked the aid area off-limits, but this man had somehow bulldozed his way through the barricade and was heading straight for Dick. What a sight to behold with his hair blowing in the wind and his flexed muscles ready for a fight.

He stopped abruptly when he arrived at the stretcher where Dick was standing. He stared Dick down for a brief moment, looked at the woman on the stretcher covered in soot, and then lost complete control. He had found his wife.

He shoved Dick aside and pounced on top of the stretcher, calling his wife's name over and over.

Dick called out to the EMTs, "Get him off! Hold him back!" But the man was going berserk. He just kept crying and screaming her name. It took four EMTs to pull him away.

Trying to help the man gain some composure, Dick pacified him. "She's going to be fine. We got to her in time, we've suctioned her out, her blood pressure is good. She has started breathing on her own. She's going to make it."

Dick looked down at the woman, and she started to stir. The husband saw her movement, too, and it brought a calm over him. Dick took her tube out and put an oxygen mask on her. After another ten or fifteen minutes, the woman was able to sit up and talk to her husband through the mask. The rugged man hugged his wife closely, sobbing and laughing at the same time.

The man, now more civil, turned to Dick and was eager to explain why he had been so hysterical. He pointed to the top of the MGM Hotel to where he and his wife had been staying. When they woke up, there was so much smoke that he knew they had to get to a lower floor as soon as possible.

"Stay here!" he had called out to his wife. "I'm going to see if we can get down the stairs. I'll come back for you."

He had crawled out into the hall, staying as low as he could, and then opened the door to the stairs, crawling down another two or three flights. Along the way, he passed the bodies of several people who had tried to descend standing up. They had been overcome with smoke inhalation and were lying unconscious. The husband had to crawl over their lifeless bodies on his way down.

He saw that the smoke was clearing on the lower floors, so he climbed back up the stairwell to get to his wife. When he got back to his floor, the stairwell door had locked behind him. In desperation he pounded on it with all his might until both hands felt like they were broken. He screamed as loudly as he could, but in the panic, no one could hear him. He kicked and threw his body up against the metal door, but it wouldn't budge.

The physical exertion had caused more smoke to fill his lungs, and he felt himself passing out. If he didn't go down, he'd die. With one last frantic kick, he pushed against the door once more. Nothing. With a curdling wail he turned and crawled down the stairs to safety. In his mind he knew he had left his wife alone in their room; most likely, she was dead. The vision of her agonizing death was driving him insane.

Still not willing to give up, he watched as every woman was carried out by the firemen. As he paced the walkway in front of the hotel, he spotted a figure resembling his wife. That's when he bound toward Dick.

By the time the man finished recounting his story, the pace had started to slow down. The firemen then resorted to carrying out the dead. Dick finally had time to look into the faces of many of the survivors—the array of emotions told a thousand stories. Dick's eyes fell on one man who looked weak and despondent. He was having difficulty breathing, but his condition was stable. For someone who had just been saved, he looked completely dejected. In situations such as these, the face tells the story of the heart. Dick asked him what had happened. The man's eyes gushed with tears.

He had come to Las Vegas to gamble with three of his buddies. They shared two rooms with a common balcony. When the fire broke out, the friends gathered in the same room and watched as the enormously thick escape ropes dropped from the roof.

The weakened man went on to explain that he had watched as the first of his three buddies climbed out onto the balcony, took hold of the rope, and held on for dear life. The man was hanging from the twenty-eighth floor with smoke billowing from the jagged window glass. He was petrified. Finally, he let himself slide an inch or two, then froze. His buddies tried to coax him to keep sliding, but within minutes, his grip gave way and he fell to his death.

In terror, the second friend ventured out on the rope, determined not to make the same mistake. He began to descend carefully. A half story down, though, he looked to the ground. Fear weakened his grip and he tumbled to the pavement. The third friend committed himself to the rope but met the same fate.

By this time, the man didn't know what he should do. He had just witnessed the graphic deaths of his closest friends. He looked behind him and contemplated the alternative—descending the steps—but the veil of smoke prevented him.

If I stay here, I'll die, he reasoned. He looked at the rope, then down over the rail. He had a choice: to commit himself to the rope or to burn. In his moment of incapable decision, he nearly jumped out of his skin as he felt a huge hand pinch his shoulder. He turned around as a fireman slapped a mask onto his face and carried him away to safety.

Only one man in the entire hotel had been able to descend on the ropes. He was an old cowboy. As he was dressing, he noticed smoke pouring in through the air conditioner. He went to the window and heard the commotion and saw the blackened sky; he knew tragedy had overtaken the hotel.

"I'm not the religious type," he told a reporter, "but I started praying."

That's when the man saw the lifeline dangling in front of the balcony to the adjoining room. The cowboy lay down on the floor and crawled out in the hall and into the next room. The people there weren't about to climb out onto that rope after seeing so many fall to their deaths. This old cowboy chanced the odds and climbed over the railing, wrapping his rough, chapped hands and scuffed boots around the rope. Then he just let himself slide. His big, leather cowboy boots took the rope burn just fine and saved his life.

When I returned from California that afternoon, the radio and television stations were reporting tragic stories as well as brave rescue attempts. But I was struck by one thought in particular: If Dick hadn't missed his first flight many months prior, he not only would have never met Morris Shenker, but he also wouldn't have been in Las Vegas, staying at the Dunes Hotel, when the MGM caught fire. As these things happen, the Dunes Hotel could have been located across town from the MGM—but no, it was right across the street. Since the main medical station ended up being smoked out, just think how many people are alive today, saved because God had diverted Dick onto a later flight several months before. These are the adventures that unfold when we give God room to work in our lives.

THE FIERY TEST

After hours of intubating dozens of smoke-stricken gamblers and tourists, Dick had put in more than a full day's work. He was exhausted. Late that afternoon, my father called Dick and asked if he would share his experiences at the crusade that night. It would prove to be a very emotional service as many of the people there knew someone who had perished.

As Dick was preparing his notes, he contemplated the difference between the eighty-seven people who died instantly in that fire and the extended chance Morris Shenker had been given. He had several opportunities to hear the gospel and consider its truth. He was blessed with years to reflect on what his near-death experience might mean. But reality is that what we do in life will be tested by fire someday. As Dick looked around at the workmanship of the hotel and considered it all, he wondered what things in his life would survive that test of fire.

First Corinthians 3:10–15 says:

> But each one should be careful how he builds. For no one can lay any foundation other than the one already laid, which is Jesus Christ. If any man builds on this foundation using gold, silver, costly stones, wood, hay or straw, his work will be shown for what it is, because the Day will bring it to light. It will be revealed with fire, and the fire will test the quality of each man's work. If what he has built survives, he will receive his reward. If it is burned up, he will suffer loss; he himself will be saved, but only as one escaping through the flames. (NIV)

To walk in sync with God, we need the right foundation. There are a lot of traps in life, a lot of potholes, so a good foundation is essential. Many people today lay a foundation in life based on good works, but good works will be consumed in the fire. They won't last.

After the MGM Hotel burned down, the glitter—like the wood, hay, and stubble—and all the plastic that had been made to look like marble or ornate woodwork, shrank and buckled in the heat and was finally consumed.

What kind of foundation are you building your life on? Are you trusting in religion, that somehow by going to church and giving money you'll build a good foundation that will please God?

There were thousands of people in the MGM Hotel, and probably many of them, by the standards of the world, would be considered good people. They weren't murderers, they paid their taxes on time, and they gave money to charity. They were patriotic and loved their country. Many never dreamed when they went to bed the night before that they would wake up in hell.

What do we put our faith, security, and trust in? American Express, "Don't Leave Home Without It," isn't going to help you here. Your ATM card won't count. Your new Ralph Lauren outfit and the party you were invited to the week before won't matter, neither will your accomplishments or your university degrees. World records that you might have set, notoriety or fame you might have attained, will be of no value, and, frankly, no one will care. What will matter is your position before God.

We all someday have to cross the river of death. To walk with God for eternity, step out on a firm foundation, Jesus Christ. *"For there is no other name under heaven given to men by which we must be saved"* (Acts 4:12 NIV).

15

HE'S COMING BACK

H E'S COMING BACK." I don't know how many times I heard
that growing up, but even today I can clearly remember my
mother saying it as I watched my father heading down the drive-
way, his taillights rounding the curve as he left for another crusade.

"He'll be back before you know it," Mama would say.

As a child, it seemed like we were asking her every day, "When
is Daddy coming back?"

"Soon," she'd say, "it won't be long, now."

Even so, it felt like forever. Soon was never soon enough. When
you're young, six weeks feels like a lifetime.

It was always hard watching my father leave, but Mama made it
tremendously exciting as we anticipated his return. When we
finally heard his tires catch the gravel in the road leading up to the
house, nothing could keep us from running down the hill to greet
him. He really did come back, just as Mama promised.

It's going to happen. He's coming back. Virtually every person
whom I respect is sure of it, and most of them are confident that it's
going to happen sooner than many of us realize: Jesus is coming back.

For some people, that's bad news. "We've got a good thing
going," they say. "Why end it? We're on a roll!"

Economically, it's hard to argue with them. America has experienced the longest period of economic growth in modern history.

The economies of Europe and Asia have been growing. It is interesting, though, that many economists believe that the end of this growth is upon us, and at the time of this writing, stocks are finally once again showing their volatility.

On a national security level, the world also looks pretty good. As a kid, I lived under the threat of nuclear holocaust. My grammar school was a fallout shelter, with a yellow-and-black civil-defense sign bolted to the side of the building, letting people know that if bombs began to fall, they could take refuge there and would have shelter, water, and food—so it was said. I'm not so sure it would have worked (the school looked like it would crumble if a firecracker went off), but that yellow-and-black sign sure made us feel good.

Who would have dreamed that within just a few years the threat of Communism and the Cold War would be a thing of the past? Ronald Reagan stood above the Berlin Wall and challenged Mikhail Gorbachev to "tear down this wall." George Bush talked about the "thousand points of light." Bill Clinton promised he could "ease our pain." Politicians want you to believe that if you put your faith and trust in them, government can help solve your problems. "Let us raise your taxes just a little bit more, and we can get the national debt under control," they tell us. People buy into that. Just because the economy is on an upswing, and our old archrival, the USSR, doesn't exist anymore, we think everything is okay.

North Korea is showing signs of conciliation toward South Korea, and even China seems to be coming around as Tiananmen Square fades into a distant memory.

We are living in the middle of an information explosion. With the use of fax machines, cell phones, cyberspace, and e-mail, information flows more freely than ever before. The Internet has opened up virtually unlimited possibilities for the dissemination and gathering of opinions, knowledge, and research.

To the unbelieving world, these are all signs of progress, all reasons why it would be a disappointment if Jesus were to return and end it all. Life is at its best; why doesn't Jesus wait until things get bad?

But what about the spiritual temperature of our nation and our world? What about the fact that, according to *U.S. News & World Report*, the United States has now become the pornography-producing capital of the world? Thanks to advancements in technology, one guy working out of his garage can produce, duplicate, and disseminate X-rated videotapes to most countries—and through the Internet, marketing can be incredibly inexpensive.

Yet instead of lamenting this, our country celebrates it! Larry Flynt, the founder of *Hustler* magazine, is somehow portrayed as a hero who defends free speech in a major motion picture release. Even some of our nation's leading politicians, in recent times, have been accused of moral misconduct, but it seems we don't care as long as politicians are perceived as doing a good job. Have we, as a nation, lost our moral conscience?

Our priorities are all mixed up. In 1997 a twelve-year-old boy was gunned down in Washington, D.C.—a victim of gang-related violence. It is not uncommon for teenagers to be murdered for their Nike shoes or their NFL team jackets.

We are more concerned about animal rights than human rights. I watched on television as rescuers risked their lives to save a moose that had fallen through the ice on a frozen lake in the northeast. TV cameras from across the state covered the rescue minute by minute. Occasionally a whale will wash up on shore, and seemingly out of nowhere people will come by the thousands to "free Willy." Yet with all the attention given to animal rights, one and a half million unborn children continue to be slaughtered each year in our country. We call this abortion—and President Clinton twice vetoed legislation designed to stop it. One day he will have to stand before God and give an account for the blood on his hands.

Sure, the world might be looking good economically and politically, but morally, we're on a sled slipping dangerously downhill.

It's moral madness. Sins that used to be hushed up—incest, gross sexual immorality, addictions, and shameful behavior—are now glorified on morning and afternoon television talk shows. Nobody's a "sinner." Everybody's a "victim."

Divorce is escalating to the degree that an entire magazine, *Divorce*, was launched in 1996 to cover the subject.

Gambling is also on the rise.

Child abuse is soaring. According to the *Kennebec Journal*, in Maine alone, the number of children under state protection has increased 41 percent since 1991.

On a moral level, things have gotten so bad that one of our presidents was reported to say, "I see no hope. There is no way we can get ourselves out of the mess we are in."

But there is hope. Jesus is coming back.

There are plenty of reasons why Christ's imminent return is good news and why it may be more sudden than we think.

QUICK TURNS

When I travel in the MU2 and have a particularly tight schedule, I will often call ahead to notify the airport that I'm coming in for fuel and need a "quick turn."

History also has its "quick turns." The year 1991 was a momentous one as world affairs unfolded at breakneck speed. Within hours after Allied Forces launched their offensive against Iraqi dictator Saddam Hussein, his supposedly powerful republican army was crushed. The Soviet Union, a nation held together for decades by repressive Communist ideology, came unraveled in a matter of weeks. The sudden change in that country startled everyone.

Just weeks after the Soviet Union collapsed, Samaritan's Purse was allowed to establish an evangelical diagnostic medical clinic in the heart of Moscow. We were given permission to conduct chapel services, distribute Bibles and Christian literature, and carry on an active program of evangelism through the clinic. This would have been unthinkable just twelve months before!

What a quick turn.

And during that same twelve-month span, after long years of frustrated negotiations, Western hostages in Lebanon emerged from captivity suddenly, as if floodgates on a dam had been forced opened. We were able to hear firsthand the accounts and ordeal of Terry Waite, Terry Anderson, and others.

Even our personal lives can change in a fleeting moment. For years a friend of mine, strong and healthy, ate all the right things and exercised. While working out one day, he died suddenly of a massive heart attack before anyone could get him to the hospital. How quickly events in life can turn.

One of the lessons we should learn from history is how quickly things that seem to be permanent can change when our sovereign, Almighty God permits it. In Revelation 22, the last chapter of the Bible, we are repeatedly warned that Christ is coming soon: *"I am coming quickly!"* (vv.12, 20).

As soon as Christ comes back, there will be no more movies glorifying the contributions of pornographers. No more children will die execution-style by doctors in sterile white coats. Life will be cherished, not cheapened or destroyed. Overnight, life as we know it will change.

A Universal Feeling

In many ways I feel that Christ has already called ahead, as I do in my MU2, warning, "I'm coming, get ready! Be prepared for a quick turn."

We should not be afraid of a quick turn in world events. Jesus has called ahead. He's told us exactly what's going to happen. His return is going to be like a flash of lightning from East to West, and it will happen when people least expect it. And when will we least expect it? When things are good. When we're on a roll. When the stock market is higher than it has ever been.

Jesus said when you hear people say, "peace, peace," watch out. Yet "peace" is all you hear today, and few seem to be on the lookout. He's called ahead. You better listen.

Jesus warned that when we hear of wars and rumors of wars, of famines and earthquakes, His return isn't far behind.

Be sure to take the right steps now to see that your walk is completely in sync with God when a quick turn rushes into your life.

He's coming, it's a fact, but instead of being alert, concerned, and expectant, our world is snoozing. We're living life as normal, as if the return of our Lord has no more consequence or relevance than the next day's delivery of unwanted mail.

My friend Ezra Sargunam of Madras, India, set a goal to build one thousand evangelical churches in India. He is dedicated to that goal, but he confessed to me, "Brother Franklin, I think Jesus could return any moment."

Sami Dagher looks at the ongoing struggle in the Middle East unlike any other man I've known. "My brother," he says, "Christ is coming back, and these wicked men can have this not-so-holy Holy Land. For me, my family, and the church in Beirut, we will be with God in heaven."

Because of their eternal perspective, these followers of Christ are working in overdrive and accomplishing much for God's kingdom. Even if Jesus delays His return by a hundred or even a thousand years, what should that be to us? Our lives will be richer for living with that expectancy.

It's this expectancy that keeps me focused and wanting to stay in sync. As His child, I long to see Him face-to-face.

While I'm waiting, I'm more aware of my walk. If my prayer life is faltering and my Bible study is on the back shelf, I know I've lost my expectancy, and with it, I've lost my focus. I need that focus to stay in sync with God: "When are you coming, Lord Jesus? When? I can't wait!"

I have this sense that the Lord Jesus is right behind the clouds. His armies are fully armed, mounted, and waiting for the final signal. As you read these pages, maybe God is pausing just long enough for me to invite you, if you don't know Him, into His Kingdom.

"Soon, Peter, soon," Jesus may be saying. "Heaven's not quite full yet. There's room for one more."

PERSONAL RETURNS

Over the years, Samaritan's Purse has been involved in many projects in Ethiopia. I have had the privilege of visiting that country and working with the churches. I remember meeting Andy Meakins, an Englishman who worked for The Evangelical Alliance Relief (TEAR) Fund, an organization based in England that works all over the world. TEAR Fund's founder, George Hoffman, worked with Samaritan's Purse in the early years.

Andy was assigned to Ethiopia. On first appearance, Andy looked like a stereotypical intellectual. He was balding, had a wiry frame, wore glasses, and had that bookworm appearance. He was always quiet and shy, but very competent in his line of expertise.

Andy was trained as a civil engineer and had helped Samaritan's Purse with a well-drilling program begun in Ethiopia. In the early eighties, he met and married an Ethiopian woman by the name of Ruth.

I had no way of knowing it at the time, but at the end of his life, Andy would display the kind of courage that is as amazing as it is inspiring.

In 1992 Andy began working in Addis Ababa as urban ministries coordinator for the Kale Heywet Church, an evangelical church in

Ethiopia that serves some three million members. Four years later, Andy was bound for the Ivory Coast on Ethiopian Airlines, one of Africa's few world-class aviation operations.

As soon as the plane reached 31,000 feet, and the seat-belt sign was turned off, three men rushed the cockpit. One carried a fire ax; another carried a fire extinguisher; the third man carried something wrapped inside a glove, which he claimed was a bomb. In his other hand, he held a bottle of Black & White blended Scotch whisky.

There was a struggle for control in the cockpit. The copilot was forced out of his chair and beaten. One of the hijackers started playing with the controls, at one point sending the plane into a dangerous dip.

"We're taking this plane to Australia," they told the captain, Leul Abate.

"But we don't have enough fuel to reach Australia! That's nine or ten hours more. It's impossible," the captain insisted. The hijackers demanded that he change his course. After several hours of flight over the Indian Ocean, the pilot recognized his plane's peril — it was about to run out of jet fuel.

The passengers were horrified when they finally heard the pilot's calm and steady voice share the terrifying news over the plane's sound system: The hijackers had forbidden him to refuel, and one engine had shut down.

"Flight attendants should prepare for a crash landing," he warned.

Up to this point the passengers had been relatively quiet, since they didn't want to agitate the hijackers. Some even continued to read their newspapers. But as soon as the pilot announced a crash landing, pandemonium erupted. The passengers realized that with little fuel remaining and hijackers threatening to blow up the plane, their chances of survival were next to nil.

Several people started sobbing. The popping sound of people prematurely inflating their life vests could be heard throughout the cabin. This action proved fatal, as many were eventually trapped under the fuselage by the air in their jackets. In that moment of stark terror, when most people were thinking of what they might possibly do to increase their chance of survival, Andy Meakins unbuckled his seat belt, stood up, and got the attention of his fellow passengers.

"Many of us might die in this crash," he admitted, "so there's something you need to know."

Andy then explained the gospel. He told his fellow passengers that God loved us so much that he sent His Son, Jesus Christ, from heaven down to this earth to take our sin away.

"Even though we may perish now on this plane," he said, "you can have that hope of eternal life."

One of the people listening to Andy's invitation was a flight attendant with Ethiopian Airlines. She quietly bowed her head, confessed to God that she was a sinner, asked Him for His forgiveness, and then asked Jesus Christ to come into her heart.

Suddenly, the airplane's last fuel-starved engine died, and there was a deathly silence as the Boeing 767 began its shaky and harrowing descent above the ocean twenty miles offshore. Andy knew that every second counted. Many people on the plane were just seconds away from eternity. He repeated his invitation with urgency: "You must receive Jesus Christ *now* into your heart by faith."

The crew began working frantically to help everyone prepare for the crash. The captain did an outstanding job, given the circumstances. He ditched the plane just several hundred yards shy of a tiny resort island in the Indian Ocean. The plane somersaulted and broke into three pieces, finally settling on a shallow reef. The front section, holding the business-class passengers, landed upright.

The sunbathing tourists and the busy staff of the luxurious Le Galawa Beach Hotel couldn't believe their eyes when out of the clear blue sky a plane silently appeared and splashed into the water surrounding the Comoros Islands. Some of the tourists thought it must be a movie stunt, but within seconds, most realized a horrible tragedy had occurred.

Some quick thinkers from the hotel staff jumped into the hotel's speedboats and headed for the wreckage as a tourist videotaped the tragic event, but only a relatively few survivors were plucked from the water. The rescuers, for the most part, ended up hauling in corpses. Just 50 people out of 175 survived.

Andy Meakins was not among the survivors, but the flight attendant who asked Christ into her heart in the doomed plane lived to tell the story of his courageous witness. In the face of death, Andy thought of others before he thought of himself. Oblivious to his own condition, he got out of his seat and used every last second of his life to give others a chance at eternal life. He could have stayed huddled in his seat, a pillow over his head, his seat belt strapped around him, doing everything he could to extend his life. Instead, he made the most out of his last few minutes of life for the sake of the gospel.

I'm sure that most people who knew Andy had opinions similar to mine: He was a competent and unselfish but relatively unremarkable man. Death proved my opinion wrong. Andy was not only a remarkable man, he was a giant of a man.

Shortly before his death, TEAR Fund had asked Andy to write an article expressing his conviction that Christians should reach out to the urban poor. In that article, Andy gave us a glimpse of his sacrificial heart: "Jesus cried over Jerusalem, but then went down to give up his life there. As followers of Jesus we should allow ourselves to cry aloud to God for our cities. Then be ready to go, directed by God, to live and speak His message of love and hope."

Andy was clearly prepared not only to live God's message of love and hope, but also to die for it. And that's what he did.

Jesus didn't end the world in Andy's lifetime, but He came for Andy at a time when Andy was not expecting it. When Andy boarded that Ethiopian Airlines flight, he had no way of knowing that a quick turn of events was getting ready to take place.

The uncle of a friend of mine recently passed away unexpectedly. On the day of his funeral, his widow was told by her doctors that she had six months or less to live. She was not expecting death. Now she knew it was coming. She had put her faith and hope in the Lord Jesus Christ. She received advanced notice of this "quick turn" and was ready.

Many of you are not ready, whether the turn is quick or slow. You haven't walked with God in the past and you're not walking with Him now. Your life is totally, 100 percent out of step with God. You have been living for yourself, for what you can get, for what you can gain.

The Bible asks, what shall it profit a man if he should gain the whole world yet lose his soul? Where's your soul going to spend eternity? Heaven or hell? God is going to win in your life in the end, whether you like it or not. It's either heaven or hell. You have to make the choice.

I'm not telling you anything I haven't faced already. When I was twenty-two years old, my parents treated me to dinner on my birthday while we were in Switzerland. Afterward, my father and I went for a walk along the lake. "Franklin," he told me, "you're going to have to make a choice either to accept Christ or reject Him. You can't continue to play the middle ground.

"I want you to know we're proud of you. We love you no matter what you do in life and no matter where you go. The door of our home is always open, and you're always welcome. But you're going to have to make a choice."

I was angry. I thought I had cleverly covered my bases and fooled my parents into thinking I had faith. I went to church. I sang the hymns. I said all the right things. But you can't fool God. He sees everything. I had to choose. I knew I couldn't pretend any longer.

Is your life in step with God's plan and purpose for you? Since none of us know the exact hour or date of our death, the only responsible attitude is one of continual watchfulness and preparedness. To those who have the attitude *"Take life easy; eat, drink and be merry,"* Jesus warns: *"You fool! This very night your life will be demanded from you. Then who will get what you have prepared for yourself?"* (Luke 12:20 NIV).

In light of this, how are we to live? Jesus tells us that the "faithful and wise servant" is the one who is living a life of expectancy, doing those things that His master has told Him to do—walking in sync with God. What are those things? They're the things that touch the heart of God: sharing the gospel (like Andy Meakins), confronting sin (like Dennis Agajanian), feeding the hungry and managing the resources God has given us (like Sami Dagher), or attending to the sick (like Aileen and Eleanor).

Jesus has called ahead warning that a quick turn is coming. Are you ready? *"Watch therefore, for you know neither the day nor the hour in which the Son of Man is coming"* (Matt. 25:13).

MARY DAMRON FREQUENTLY entertains herself and others by singing primitive mountain music. On our trip to Bosnia, she taught all of us, including Ricky Skaggs, a song she particularly likes. When I think of Mary, I find myself humming the tune—sometimes even singing each verse. But without the twang that mountain singers have perfected, it doesn't sound quite the same. The song tells about how life sometimes takes us up on the mountain, but it can also take us down into the dark valleys. It reminds us that the God on the mountain is also the God in the valley. He's the God of the good and bad times, and the God of the day is still God in the night.

There's a lot of truth in this song. Many of us are mountaintop Christians. We think we'll stay in sync with God as long as He keeps us on the highest plateau. But when we get used to the good times, we forget all about God. We don't have time for Him any more.

Yet all of us inevitably come tumbling off that mountaintop and land in the depths—the valleys of illness, depression, financial insecurity, family feuds, temptation, and sin. We've all been in them. Those are the moments when we are tempted to question God's love and provision.

And yet, if we truly want to live a life beyond the limits, we need something that will keep us in step with Him, whether we're on top of a high mountain or walking in the shadows of the valley of death. That "something" is faith.

One of my favorite passages of Scripture has always been Hebrews 11. It begins by defining faith: *"Now faith is the substance of things hoped for, the evidence of things not seen. For by it the elders obtained a good testimony"* (vv.1–2).

You see, that's what I want in life: a good testimony. I want to hear my heavenly Father say, *"Well done, thou good and faithful servant."*

The book of Hebrews tells us how we can build an ironclad testimony:

> *By faith Abel offered to God a more excellent sacrifice than Cain, through which he obtained witness that he was righteous, God testifying of his gifts; and through it he being dead still speaks.* (11:4)

Imagine that. *Being dead, Abel still speaks.* How many people wear themselves out trying to achieve some sort of earthly immortality? People try to amass great wealth, achieve unparalleled fame, or set world records, just so that there will be some evidence that they existed. Politicians want to leave their mark on history. Only a few do, like George Washington, Abraham Lincoln, and Ronald Reagan. Most fade into obscurity, and their speeches and legislation are forgotten.

I understand their drive and their search for significance, but they are depositing their efforts in the wrong bank. Putting all your money and effort into an earthly inheritance is like investing in horses and buggies—the future will leave you behind. Our future— the one that counts—is in heaven. It is called life everlasting: *"The earth will grow old like a garment, and those who dwell in it will die in like manner; but My salvation will be forever, and My righteousness will not be abolished"* (Isa. 51:6). And in eternity, faith is the only currency that counts.

Hebrews 11:6 goes on to say, *"Without faith it is impossible to please Him, for he who comes to God must believe that He is, and that He is a rewarder of those who diligently seek Him."* You can be the most religious person in your town and go to church every time the door is open. But if you don't have faith, you're just play-acting the Christian life.

The problem in many of our churches today is that we have lost our faith.

But you see, Hebrews 11 tells us that it was faith that kept Noah in sync with God. When the skies were still clear, Noah got on board, didn't he?

It was faith that moved Abraham to go to a foreign country and later offer up his only son, Isaac. By putting Isaac on the altar, Abraham knew he was putting everything on the line—how could God's promise come true if Abraham sacrificed his only true heir? But Abraham's faith moved him to be obedient—he stayed in sync with God's will and purpose.

Faith leads to action.

How can we have the kind of faith that is never shaken, questioned, or doubted?

Zero Hour Faith

Over the years, I have been privileged to meet people of tremendous faith. Some of the great missionaries I have known have lived extraordinary lives of faith. My grandfather Dr. L. Nelson Bell left Virginia's Shenandoah Valley right after World War I to go to China, where he spent the next twenty-five years serving the Chinese people in Christ's name.

In the mid-eighties, I had a chance to go to China with my mother and father. Today in that country, there are literally tens of thousands of Christians who can trace their faith back to my grandfather's ministry as a medical missionary. When he died after many years of service to our Lord, he didn't leave his family a great wealth of earthly possessions, but what a remarkable testimony and example he left behind for his children and grandchildren.

A good friend of mine, Dr. Bob Foster, is also a man of faith. Though a Canadian citizen, Bob grew up in Africa. As a young man, Bob believed God called him to become a medical missionary. Being from a missionary family presented a major hurdle, though. He had no money.

Even so, convinced that God was calling him, Bob persevered and applied the principles of faith he had seen his parents put into practice. At seventeen, Bob completed the application to medical school. He asked the Lord to supply the fee. He waited and waited and waited some more, but not one dollar came.

As the second hand ticked closer to the deadline hour, Bob decided to submit his application—minus the fee.

Standing in line at the university, he shoved his hands down into his empty pockets and wondered where he would get his fees. He knew God had called him to be a missionary doctor. Even though two fingers had been crushed while working at a shipyard that summer, trying to earn enough money for his registration and tuition fees, God had allowed his fingers to be partially saved. To him, that was proof God wanted him to continue pursuing his dream to become a doctor. As the line moved slowly forward, Bob grew anxious—if he only had $450.

"What's your name?" the registrar interrupted his thoughts as he stepped up to the desk.

"Robert Livingstone Foster," he replied nervously.

He watched as she ran her finger down a list of names, then stopped and looked up at him.

"Your bill has been paid. You won a scholarship from your high school exams, and the money has already been credited to your account. All your fees have been taken care of for the year."

Stunned, Bob walked away with an overwhelming sense of gratitude. There was no doubt in his mind that God had prepared him for medical school and He was going to pay the bills as well. In fact, in the years ahead, Bob saw such provision over and over again. Several years, he received scholarships for scholastic achievement. Three years after the accident at the shipyard, Workmen's Compensation called, telling him that they had made an award to him for permanent disability. The amount covered a full year of medical school.

This was a pattern that seemed to follow Bob throughout his medical training. He found himself having to wait until zero hour when God would miraculously provide desperately needed funds in order to continue. Through the grace and provision of his heavenly Father, Bob finished medical school and set his sights on the mission field. God was developing his character and faith for the adventures he would come to experience in another part of the world.

Like his parents, Bob has served God in some of the most difficult places throughout Africa. He raised seven children on the mission field, and many of them today are serving the Lord in foreign countries. In his retirement he stays busier than ever, raising money for mission projects, traveling to Africa to relieve missionary doctors so that they can have time off, and preaching Christ at every opportunity. Without faith exercised and proven, Bob would never have accomplished on earth what God intended. He experienced firsthand what the book of James tells us:

> The testing of your faith develops perseverance. Perseverance must finish its work so that you may be mature and complete, not lacking anything. (1:3–4 NIV)

To have faith like Bob Foster, we're going to have to confront the enemies of faith.

The Enemies of Faith

One enemy of faith is our *possessions.* Abraham was willing to put everything on the line because *"he waited for the city which has foundations, whose builder and maker is God"* (Heb. 11:10). We're not willing to wait. We want everything, and we want it *now.* Many times God provides on the last day or at the last hour, sometimes at the very last minute.

Think of the blessing Bob would have missed had he refused to deliver his application because he didn't have the money needed! What Bob did not know as he stood in line was that God had already provided days before.

I understand the lure of possessions and enticing desires. We all feel their tug. And if we're not careful, they can pull us down. I remember when Jane Austin and I were first married and we could load everything we owned in her little Ford Maverick. I recall the freedom of being packed and on the road in ten minutes. It was great! Nothing to hold us back.

Though most of us do not live as nomads, we still need to ask, *Is my faith being buried by my possessions? Is my faith shattered most when my financial situation looks the bleakest? Do I define my security by what I have stored in the bank?* By themselves, possessions aren't sinful, but our faith is buried when we begin to worship things. *"Take heed and beware of covetousness, for one's life does not consist in the abundance of the things he possesses"* (Luke 12:15).

Another enemy of faith is *experience.* We limit ourselves by what we think is humanly possible. Hebrews 11:11 tells us that *"By faith Sarah herself also received strength to conceive seed, and she bore a child when she was past the age, because she judged Him faithful who had promised."* How could a woman past the age of childbearing conceive and give birth to a son? That's humanly impossible—but faith points to a God for whom nothing is too hard.

When Bob Pierce started Samaritan's Purse, people thought his vision of immediate response to the world's most urgent needs was brilliant, but practically impossible. Bureaucracy would get in the way. Business meetings would block the flow of critically needed funds. Red tape would strangle his good intentions. People didn't believe in Bob's vision because they had never seen it done—a relief organization that could move quickly, immediately, and commit to providing aid virtually on the spot. People scoffed.

But Bob's vision has grown many times over in the years since. God has created a way for relief to begin flowing when and where it's needed—not just months after a lengthy approval process. Bob blew the limits that kept many others back.

One of the devil's favorite excuses is, "But that's never been done. Why try?" The faithful Christian's answer is, "If God's really calling us to do this, He'll provide a way to get it done."

Possibly the greatest lesson I learned from Bob Pierce was something he called *God room*. This was a phrase he coined that simply means recognizing a need bigger than what human limitations can meet. Yet you press on to meet the need that you believe God has placed on your heart; trust Him to close the gap and watch a miracle unfold by God's own provision. Before you know it, the need is met through ways that seem completely impossible.

Bob always told me, "Faith isn't required as long as you set your goal only as high as the most intelligent, most informed, and expert human efforts can reach. You don't exercise faith until you have committed more than it's possible to give." Bob Foster's story illustrates this principle so well.

I like how Charles Wesley defined faith:

> Faith, mighty faith, the promise sees,
> And looks to God alone;
> Laughs at impossibilities,
> And cries it shall be done.

Faith is the power that God gives us to break out of our human limitations and become the people He created us to be. Use this power to slay the enemies of faith and experience the joy of living in sync with Him.

NAME ON THE LINE

"I'VE GOT TO CALL MEL," I thought. Samaritan's Purse had been working in Bosnia and Croatia during their civil war in the early nineties, and the television screen in front of me was throwing out images of hospitals with blood flowing out the front doors. Men, women, and children were lying in rows in the corridors. Civilians and soldiers moaning, others dying on camera, as they waited for help that in many cases never came in time.

Dr. Melvin Cheatham, a neurosurgeon and my good friend, was a natural choice to help repair some of the broken bodies ripped apart by the Bosnian civil war. I had personally seen many gruesome accounts of heads being split open and spinal cords being pierced, and I knew of no one more qualified than Mel Cheatham to put these fragile bodies back together. I also knew of no doctor more eager to take the message of Jesus Christ to people who had lost all hope. Mel's book, *Living a Life that Counts*, has been a great inspiration to me and to thousands of others.

I picked up the phone, having no idea that I was setting in motion a series of events that would tell the gospel story in a courageous display of love.

In spite of the danger, Mel agreed to go. He only had one request: "Can I take Sylvia [his wife of thirty-eight years] with me?"

"By all means," I told him, surprised that she would even consider such a trip.

By committing to lead the Samaritan's Purse team into Bosnia, Mel knew he would be exposing both himself and his wife to all the dangers that come with war. It's one thing to make a decision to enter a country in the midst of civil war when you're tucked safely away in your quiet home in Ventura, California, overlooking the deep blue Pacific Ocean. It's another thing altogether to follow through on that decision when you hear the sounds of war greeting your descent into what at the time was the most dangerous airport in the world, Sarajevo.

It was no easy task to get the Cheathams into Bosnia. First, we had to secure United Nation Identification Cards. To do this, we had to fly them into Croatia, where they would state their reason and mission for travel and register with the UN, then apply with them for a flight into Sarajevo. The United Nations had kept the airport in Sarajevo open for their humanitarian flights, using C-130 cargo planes, but the UN was powerless to stop the snipers and random artillery fire that greeted each landing plane. Accordingly, the UN required Mel and his wife to wear Kevlar helmets and bulletproof body armor, weighing about sixty pounds each.

Mel is a slender, medium-built man in his early sixties. He is a quiet, gentle, but very persuasive individual with a compassionate heart. When Mel put his bulletproof armor and his Kevlar helmet on, he looked as though he was ready for battle. Sylvia, on the other hand, is a beautiful, small, and petite woman—every inch an English lady. But when she put sixty pounds of body armor on, and that heavy-duty helmet, she looked somewhat like a human turtle. She could barely move under the weight.

The earsplitting sounds of artillery shells exploding near the plane as it made a quick turn at Sarajevo's international airport shook the passengers inside. It was a bitterly cold, cloudy, and rainy afternoon as Mel and Sylvia's United Nations cargo plane finally came to a halt. When the aircraft doors opened, the cargo load-master yelled "Run!"

Run? Mel and Sylvia looked at each other. *Under all this weight?* They grabbed their luggage, rushed across the rain-soaked tarmac, and dashed inside a bunker as another artillery round exploded, shaking the ground under their feet. The bunker, high berms of earth surrounded by sandbags and steel barriers, wasn't much, but it was sufficient to keep out the incessant sniper fire—provided that those inside kept their heads down. Mel and Sylvia could hear the bullets whizzing past their bunker. They had no desire to become better acquainted with the flying ammunition, so they waited patiently.

Mel and Sylvia were risking their lives, their health, and their safety, all for the hope that some might be won to Christ. As a neurosurgeon, Mel's livelihood depended upon his ability to use his hands. A single stray bullet could put him on permanent disability in an instant. Even so, Mel was willing to go beyond the limits of safety—all the way to Sarajevo.

If Bob Pierce were still living, he would definitely say, "Mel's got guts for Jesus."

Mel and Sylvia, and those with them, waited until the cover of darkness fell. Then, when the signal was given, UN soldiers jumped out of the bunker and fanned the surrounding area with their guns, their fingers on the triggers. In the absence of sniper fire, the Cheathams quickly escaped into an armored personnel carrier.

In many hospitals in the United States, a neurosurgeon is considered king of the hill. Mel had earned enough money so that he and Sylvia could have easily afforded to stay at any of the world's finest resorts. Instead, they spent that night hunkered down on a cold cement floor at a UN military compound surrounded by sandbags and barbed wire.

In the morning, Mel found himself at the door of the "hospital" that would be his home for the next several weeks. In fact, the original hospital had been blown to pieces and the locals had gathered every scrap of equipment and any supplies they could find and transferred them to the basement of a monastery. Mel gasped at the sight of stacks of machine guns and automatic weapons that were pushed up against the hospital wall. The symbols of war surrounded them.

Inside the hospital, wounded bodies filled the beds, hallways, and corners. Mel tried not to be bothered by the dirty linoleum floor, but it was more difficult to ignore the malaise created by the fact that the building was cold, the light was dim, and the air was heavy.

Mel and Sylvia spent the first morning walking from ward to ward, passing row upon row of twisted and maimed bodies. Some people were in comas; others had bloodstained bandages wrapped around their heads. Even though both Mel and Sylvia were well acquainted with medical emergencies, the sight of so many severed limbs and disfigured bodies was excruciatingly grim. The few conscious patients just stared ahead into space, glazed looks clouding their eyes.

Mel knew that many of these patients were going to die unless someone helped them right away. The hospital had six hundred beds and was over capacity with fifteen hundred patients, many of whom needed immediate surgery to remove pieces of shrapnel from their brains or spines. But before Mel and Sylvia arrived, there was just one neurosurgeon serving the entire hospital, a thin and gaunt-faced man named Dr. Jurisic Josip.

Dr. Josip had not always been so frail. He had lost over sixty pounds of weight in eighteen months simply because there wasn't enough food to go around. He couldn't bear to see the patients go hungry and would often sacrificially offer up his own meal rations to hungry patients.

Mel judged Dr. Josip to be a contemporary. He was astonished to learn that this overworked doctor was just thirty-nine years old. The fact that he had aged so quickly wasn't surprising, considering the patient load he was under. The war never slowed down; the flow of casualties was endless. Though patients came in on stretchers, many of them were carried out in black body bags.

Dr. Josip's English was broken but passable, and in the midst of twelve- to fifteen-hour days with Mel Cheatham, a true friendship was born. Mel was amazed as he watched Dr. Josip work, many times in clear line of sniper fire. His only source of illumination was often a flashlight, and he had to perform difficult and risky surgery in the midst of shelling and frequent power outages.

A CRINKLED PHOTOGRAPH

In a rare moment when both doctors were free, Mel asked Dr. Josip what motivated him. Dr. Josip quietly pulled out a crinkled photograph and handed it to Mel.

He looked at the photograph of Dr. Josip saying good-bye to his little boy and his wife who was expecting their second child. The two were being evacuated from Sarajevo at the beginning of the war. Dr. Josip's hand was pressed against the bus window, and on the other side of the window was pressed the tiny hand of his son. The yearning in the little boy's face broke Mel's heart. It was evident that the little boy wanted nothing more than to jump through that window and into his daddy's arms.

Separated from his son by not more than a thin piece of glass, Dr. Josip fought the tears that mercilessly filled his eyes. He had seen enough of war to realize that there was no point in making promises. He figured he would never see his son again.

After that photograph was taken, the bus lunged forward, sending a cloud of exhaust high into the air. Dr. Josip stepped out into the road behind the bus and watched it disappear.

In the days and weeks that followed, patients started to arrive from all directions, each one in seemingly worse condition than the one before. Dr. Josip realized that nothing could be done for many of them. Others would require extensive operations. The long hours dulled his own pain, though they were never sufficient to erase it. Work kept the tears away, and Dr. Josip worked harder than any surgeon Mel had ever seen.

When Mel looked at this dedicated man, all he could see was the image of the photograph. He realized that Dr. Josip was committed to returning sons to their fathers and fathers to their sons. He was saving every life he could, trying to snatch yet one more soul from the malicious jaws of war.

A Flashlight Operation

Shortly after Mel arrived, a young man in critical condition was carried into the hospital. He had been shot and was paralyzed from the neck down. The young man was an Islamic holy warrior, a member of the Mujahedin, and his friends were at the point of hysteria.

Sylvia held a flashlight as Mel examined the patient, and to his dismay discovered that the bullet had severed the spinal cord. This young man would never walk again, but Mel believed he could still live.

After several hours of extensive surgery, Mel patched up his patient the best he could and put the young warrior on a respirator.

That night, the man in charge of the generator forgot to fill it with diesel. An hour or two past midnight, the generator ground to a sudden halt, and power was cut off to the young man's lifeline.

He died within minutes.

The next morning Mel was examining another patient when Dr. Josip pulled him aside. There were no safe places to talk; even the patients might repeat a conversation that could lead to a retaliatory execution. So in a suppressed manner, Dr. Josip told Mel the bad news.

"The young warrior you operated on yesterday died during the night. The generator failed."

Mel was shocked. "I'm so sorry. That young man could have

lived." He studied Dr. Josip's troubled eyes. Still, Mel was puzzled. Patients were dying by the hour. Why was Dr. Josip pulling him aside to tell him that one particular patient had died? Couldn't it have waited?

"Dr. Cheatham," Dr. Josip went on.

Mel sensed by the tone of his voice something was dreadfully wrong.

Dr. Josip hung his head.

"Dr. Cheatham, I fear for you."

"Me? Why?"

"When the young man's fanatical friends discover he is dead, I fear they will come looking for you. The surgery log shows that you are the one who operated on him. I'm afraid that they will blame you for his death and take your life in exchange for his."

Mel was stunned, but before he could fully react, Dr. Josip added, "I have erased your name as the surgeon and have written my name in its place."

Mel looked into Dr. Josip's eyes. His mouth became dry. He felt a lump in his throat grow so large he couldn't possibly swallow it away.

"But surely, my friend," Mel protested, "that means they will come for you and kill you."

"You can leave this place of war. I cannot," Dr. Josip quickly urged. "I am prepared to die in your place if I must, in order that you might live."

Mel couldn't help but think of John 15:13: *"Greater love has no one than this, that he lay down his life for his friends"* (NIV).

As he looked at Dr. Josip holding the surgery log, he thought of the great physician, Jesus Christ, who willingly died for all.

HE TOOK MY PLACE

In all my travels, I've yet to hear of a clearer word-picture of what Jesus Christ did for us on Calvary's cross. You see, because of our sins, there is a contract of death written on our souls. Christ stepped forward and offered Himself in our place.

What Christ did surpasses even Dr. Josip's actions. Dr. Josip was willing to die for a good man. After all, Mel had risked his life to help Dr. Josip and his people.

Christ died for the unrighteous:

> At just the right time, when we were still powerless, Christ died for the ungodly. Very rarely will anyone die for a righteous man, though for a good man someone might possibly dare to die. But God demonstrates his own love for us in this: While we were still sinners, Christ died for us. (Rom. 5:6–8 NIV)

Friend, there is a judgment day ahead for all of us, and we are going to have to give an account.

As far as the young soldiers looking for Mel were concerned, Mel was not justified in their sight. He was worthy of death. But someone intervened on his behalf.

That's what Christ did for us. We have failed. We need a Savior to take our place and intercede on our behalf. Jesus Christ is *the* Savior, the only One willing to take our sin and our guilt.

But we must accept His offer. Salvation isn't automatic — for anyone. I don't get into heaven just because my father is Billy Graham. Mother Teresa doesn't get into heaven just because she's helped so many poor people. Dr. Josip doesn't get to heaven because of his sacrificial service to others. In fact, you may be interested in knowing Dr. Josip's outcome.

He survived the war and now serves as the chief of neurosurgery at the State Hospital in Sarajevo, the capital of Bosnia. In 1996 I had the privilege of dedicating the new intensive care unit that had been outfitted by Samaritan's Purse with thousands of dollars worth of medical equipment donated by Christian friends from America and Canada. Most of the assembled hospital staff, predominantly

Muslim, heard the message of God's love that had prompted the donation. They listened intently. Some faces tightened up as I spoke, but many eyes filled with tears. At the conclusion, most of them came to shake my hand and thank me for the message. Because of what Samaritan's Purse had done for this hospital and because of Mel Cheatham's service, our friendship with Dr. Josip flourished.

In the fall of 1997 we invited Dr. Josip to the United States to attend a conference I host each year at the Billy Graham Training Center in Asheville, North Carolina. The conference is called Prescription for Renewal. Most of the participants are physicians and are given the opportunity to earn medical credits, experience Christian fellowship, and hear some of the best Bible teachers in the world. Following the conference, Dr. Josip paid a visit to Samaritan's Purse headquarters in Boone. Dr. Richard Furman invited several of us to his home one evening. Skip Heitzig, pastor of Calvary Chapel in Albuquerque, New Mexico, serves on the Samaritan's Purse board of directors and was there along with many others who had attended the conference. As Dr. Josip looked around the room filled with people from many walks in life, he seemed overwhelmed. Skip and I were standing with him. He turned and said, "Something is different about your kind of Christianity—it seems real to you. I wish I had what is so evident in your lives. It seems that my church is empty but your faith is alive. What is the difference?"

Skip seized the opportunity to answer the eternal question and Dr. Josip's eyes were fixed on Skip as he shared his testimony. He, too, had been raised in a fine Roman Catholic home, but as a young man in his twenties, he began drinking alcohol and experimenting with drugs. He drifted farther from the things of God.

One night while alone at his brother's house, he flipped on the television and began surfing the channels for something to help pass the time. He came across a Billy Graham telecast and went to the refrigerator for a beer. He flopped down in a chair, popped the cap, and within minutes found himself spellbound by the message.

He heard it explained that all men are born into sin and that no one is righteous before God. Sin separates us from God, but "*God so loved the world that he gave his one and only Son, that whoever believes in him shall not perish but have eternal life*" (John 3:16 NIV).

"That night," Skip continued, "I realized that I was a sinner in need of a Savior—I wanted forgiveness. I got down on my knees, confessed my sin to God, asked Him to forgive me, and invited Jesus Christ into my heart by faith. I was forgiven and cleansed that moment and born into God's kingdom. He gave me a new start. He gave me a new life."

With tears filling his eyes, Dr. Josip patted his chest. "This is what I want. I want that same relationship with God. I want to know I am forgiven. I want to be a child of God."

By this time, everyone in the room sensed what was happening. Skip put his hand on Dr. Josip's shoulder. "Would you like to invite Jesus Christ into your heart?"

With a smile, Dr. Josip said tenderly, "Oh yes."

Skip turned to me and asked me to lead in prayer. "Dr. Josip," I said, as we all huddled close, "just repeat this simple prayer after me—God will hear us."

He bowed his head. "Dear God, I know I am a sinner. I am sorry for my sin. Forgive me. I believe that the Lord Jesus Christ, Your Son, died on Calvary's cross for my sins and that You raised Him from the grave. I want to invite Christ into my heart and live for Him as my Lord and Savior from this day forward, in Jesus name. Amen."

Dr. Josip looked up with a glow on his face. He put his arms around Skip. "Thank you for telling me about this great salvation." He embraced me. "Thank you, Franklin, for praying with me." Then he turned to Dick. "God bless you, Dr. Furman, for making your home available for such a special night as this."

As I drove home that evening, I couldn't help but rejoice

because of what Jesus Christ had done in this man's life. The change in Dr. Josip's life seemed to be almost instantaneous. The emptiness that he had a few moments earlier was replaced with joy and peace. Dr. Josip will be in heaven one day.

How about you? Where do you stand before a holy God? Are you forgiven? If you were to die now would your soul immediately go into the presence of Almighty God? You may say, "I think so." Well, I'm not talking about thinking so. I'm talking about knowing so—beyond any shadow of a doubt. Is that the kind of assurance you have?

If not, please don't close this book without being certain. Maybe you're asking, "What do I need to do?" You must be willing to confess your sin. Perhaps you're saying, "But doesn't God already know that I'm a sinner?" Yes, God is all-knowing. But He wants to hear you confess your sin to Him. You have to be willing to turn from your sin, which is repentance, and ask God's forgiveness and by faith believe that Jesus Christ died for your sins and that on the third day God raised Him from the grave. If you do this, you will receive God's forgiveness and eternal life. Then, and only then, will you experience life beyond the limits. You will live life at a new level you never dreamed possible.

God loves you and has a plan and purpose for your life. Trust Him. He wants to free you from the bondage of sin. The Bible says, "*Trust in the* LORD *with all your heart and lean not on your own understanding; in all your ways acknowledge Him, and He shall direct your paths*" (Prov. 3:5–6).

If you want Jesus to come into your heart and give you life eternal, pray the prayer I prayed with Dr. Josip, and write to me at:

Samaritan's Purse
P.O. Box 3000
Boone, NC 28607

Let me know of your decision. I would like to send you some literature, at no cost, to help you grow in your new life with Jesus Christ.

Let me encourage you to read and study the Bible, God's Word. Obey Him and watch Him take you beyond the limits of this world and into a life fully in sync with God.

AN AVID OUTDOORSMAN and pilot, Franklin Graham is President of Samaritan's Purse, a Christian relief and evangelism organization, and also First Vice-Chairman of the Billy Graham Evangelistic Association. He is the author of the bestselling autobiography, *Rebel with a Cause,* the children's book, *Miracle in a Shoebox,* and *Bob Pierce: This One Thing I Do.* He lives with his wife and children in Boone, North Carolina.

ALSO, ENJOY FRANKLIN GRAHAM'S PERSONAL STORY IN

Rebel with a Cause
An Autobiography

President of Samaritan's Purse and son of acclaimed evangelist Billy Graham, Franklin Graham offers his life story, from his childhood through his rebellious teenage years to his ministry of today in this inspiring autobiography.

0-7852-7915-6 • Hardcover • 336 pages + 16 pages of photos

0-7852-7170-8 • Trade Paper • 336 pages + 16 pages of photos